Swarthmore Lecture 1974

PROPHETS AND RECONCILERS:
reflections on the
Quaker Peace Testimony

by Wolf Mendl

FRIENDS HOME SERVICE COMMITTEE · LONDON

First published August 1974

BX
7748
W 2
M 46

© Wolf Mendl
Friends Home Service Committee
Friends House, Euston Road, London, NW1 2BJ

ISBN 0 85245 115 6

Cover design by John Blamires
Back cover photo by Norman Marrow

Printed in Great Britain in 10/12 Times
By Headley Brothers Ltd., 109 Kingsway
London, WC2B 6PX and Ashford, Kent

PREFACE

The Swarthmore Lectureship was established
by the Woodbrooke Extension Committee at a
meeting held December 9th, 1907 : the minute
of the Committee providing for 'an annual
lecture on some subject relating to the message
and work of the Society of Friends'. The name
Swarthmore was chosen in memory of the
home of Margaret Fox, which was always open
to the earnest seeker after Truth, and from
which loving words of sympathy and
substantial material help were sent to fellow
workers.

The lectureship has a twofold purpose ; first, to
interpret further to the members of the Society
of Friends their message and mission ; and,
secondly, to bring before the public the spirit,
the aims and fundamental principles of the
Friends. The lecturer alone is responsible for
any opinions expressed.

The Lectures have usually been delivered at the
time of assembly of London Yearly Meeting
of the Society of Friends. The present Lecture
in abridged form, was delivered in the
Central Hall, University of York, on the
evening of August 18th, 1974.

In 1966 the Friends Home Service Committee
took over the publication of the Swarthmore
Lectures from George Allen & Unwin Ltd., who
had published them for many years.

CONTENTS

In memory of my Mother
who introduced me to the Society of Friends

FOREWORD

The Quaker stand against all war and violence, known as the Peace Testimony, arose naturally from the religious experience of Friends. Alongside all the other 'testimonies',* it was an organic part of the central Quaker message. The founders of the movement were not very conscious of having specific testimonies about this or that. Everything they did and said stemmed from the dictates of Christ, who lived in their hearts. In the course of time, the Society of Friends became an organized body with a distinctive approach to life. The Peace Testimony formed part of it. As the problems of war became more pressing and serious with the development of the modern nation state and its military establishment, many Friends saw this as the most important witness the Society had to offer.

With the decline of traditional religion and the rise of rationalistic interpretations of the world, there came the danger that the Peace Testimony would acquire an autonomous existence and become the expression of an ideology called pacifism. This ideology has two basic components: the belief that it is desirable to settle international disputes peacefully and the belief that it is always possible to do so. Few, if any, would disagree with the first proposition. Very many would question the second. The weakness of those who believe that international quarrels can be settled without war is their tendency to ignore the realities of personal and social conflict and to think in terms of a simple panacea to remove the causes of war. The events of the first half of this century have undermined the self-confidence of many pacifists.

We now live in an age of pessimism about man's ability to create an ideal society. We no longer believe in simple solutions to social and political problems. Quakers have something to offer in such a world. They have a fundamental vision of the unity of all life and they try to realize it in the activities of small groups which are the core of the Society of Friends. The Meeting for Worship, at its best, is an open-ended fellowship of people who seek to deepen their lives in the spirit of God and who care for each other in that spirit. It is also a home from which its members go out to all kinds of activities in the service of the world. Among them are

* From earliest times, Friends were concerned with all kinds of social problems and had 'testimonies' about such matters as integrity in business, capital punishment, dress, 'hat honour', oaths, plain language, etc. Some of them are still observed today, others have become irrelevant and have fallen into desuetude.

many who will devote their efforts to the problems of conflict and violence at all levels. Their work is the subject of this essay.

Anyone writing the Swarthmore lecture labours under a double handicap. He cannot hope to do more than speak in very general terms within so small a compass, and generalizations inevitably oversimplify and may distort the truth. Secondly, he is asked to address simultaneously the Society of Friends and a wider public. This means that what I have to say will include much that is familiar and commonplace to Friends and much that may sound obscure to those who are not well acquainted with the Society.

May I be forgiven for the shortcomings of this exercise and express the hope that it will be none the less of some interest and that it may stimulate further thought and reflection among its readers.

I owe a warm word of thanks to two groups of people. One must remain nameless for it consists of all those who at some time in my life influenced me through their wisdom and enthusiasm.

The other, smaller group, includes those who have had some share in preparing this lecture. George Gorman and Barrie Paskins read the whole, Adam Roberts, Ian Roy and Richenda Scott read parts of an earlier version of the manuscript. They have helped me greatly with their criticisms and suggestions. Edward Milligan and the staff at the Library of Friends House gave invaluable and generous assistance in meeting requests for documents and information. Special thanks are due to Professor Takeshi Ishida for kindly allowing me to reproduce the Table on p. 83. My wife typed the final draft, acted as a foil for some of my ideas and served as a buffer against outside pressures while I was engaged in writing.

Wolf Mendl

*   *   *

I

THE ROOTS OF THE PEACE TESTIMONY

As a small boy I had an extensive toytown—one of those collections of charming and colourful houses, trees, fences, people, animals, railways and cars, carved out of wood as only German craftsmen could do. It afforded me endless hours of delight. My play was alternately constructive and destructive. Great care and pains were taken in building it up and in recreating the daily life of a small town. But every so often there had to be a disaster: storm or flood, war or riot, and large parts of the town were laid waste. After that I would enjoy the task of rebuilding.

There are good psychological and sociological explanations for a child's play. He recreates his environment in fantasy and he is urged on by impulses which are both constructive and destructive. As I grew up I lost my interest in this activity but I was disturbed to find—and am still disturbed—that the constructive and destructive impulses continue to be strong in me. They take different forms and are sometimes expressed in a generalized feeling towards the world.

After reading the newspaper, for instance, I can be overcome by feelings of rage and hate against everybody and everything. The same feelings arise when someone does something better than I, or receives recognition which I want to have. Then they are directed against the individual and wholly inexcusable. After drinking in a beautiful view or finishing an arduous task, I am filled with a warm and loving feeling towards the universe. Both sentiments are genuine at the moment of sensation. When angry I want to do things which are not expected of good Quakers. When content I want to do good, make someone happy, reconcile enemies.

The manifestation of these changes of mood may arise from some quirk of my psyche, but I am sure that all of us experience satisfaction and restlessness, good will and anger, love and hate, and that it points to a fundamental truth about our human condition. As in electricity, we each have within us the positive and negative. Moreover, just as the process of electrification is one of creating an electronic unbalance between the negative electrons and the positive nucleus of the atom, which releases a force that in turn corrects it, so the tension between the positive and negative in our personalities produces a continuing inner dialectic which has the effect of determining our actions. Anthropologists and psychologists study the roots of our impulses and the phenomenon of human aggression with its positive and negative functions.[1] It is left to the philosophers, moralists and religious thinkers to ponder the meaning of our actions in terms of right and wrong, good and evil.

Our emotions and feelings are conditioned by the learning process which goes on throughout life. We think that some action is good because society accepts it as such. The social environment establishes norms of conduct which are exceedingly difficult to defy. But the norms of what is good and bad may differ as between one society and another. In her study of primitive communities, Margaret Mead has shown how one cultural and educational pattern in a community can lead to gentle and friendly behaviour, whereas a different pattern can have the opposite effect and lead to aggressive and hostile behaviour among members of another community.

Our own society and the dominant culture pattern of the world seem to put a premium on competition, self-assertiveness and the acquisition of power, whether in the form of material wealth or status. Yet, in every generation many have challenged the prevalent norms and have tried to find some new way of life in which cooperation, self-denial and the sharing of wealth and authority take their place. Although these efforts to build a new society have never been wholly successful, they have established practices which have become the accepted standards. The duty of a community to care for its weaker members—the young, the old, the mentally and physically handicapped, the materially needy—is one example. The almost universal condemnation of slavery is another. The refusal to permit uncontrolled competition for material wealth or other forms of power within society is a third. The acceptance of these norms does not, alas, imply their full application. Every society falls far short of its own standards and among states there seem to be few standards other than the degree of power to protect one's own interests and to impose one's will on others.

One explanation for the persistent search for a new morality, in spite of the failures or part-failures of the past, may lie in awareness of some inner authority which compels us to follow another guide than conventional practice. To return to the personal feelings of love and hate: If I ask myself why I am frustrated and angry, I have to admit that the answer is not confined to the objective circumstances in which I find myself and the impact of society, but must also be sought in my own feelings of pride, envy and greed. When I am satisfied, it is not only because of a sense of personal achievement but also because of a sense of rising above self, when others matter more than I, when I have the sensation of being part of something greater than myself, when the *I* does not matter so much. Then I am but a link in the chain of love that binds the world; but chains, unfortunately, can also rust.

The mature person accepts the presence of conflicting impulses and emotions in his make-up and seeks to harness them in such a way that the positive and creative elements will be dominant, though not without a struggle against the negative and destructive. I would go further and suggest that the struggle is essential for personal growth and development, provided one does not become saddled with a debilitating sense of guilt. Thus, many great works of art have had their origins in an awareness of the darker side of life, even a fascination or love for evil. In social activities it is essential that we are conscious of both the positive and negative in human nature. To ignore the negative leads to superficiality in understanding the affairs of men and to futile utopianism. To ignore the positive leads to depravity in personal conduct and a nihilism in society. Among the religious-minded it results in a concentration solely on personal salvation which has little social relevance.

The Society of Friends is a religious body and its members therefore relate the phenomena of the human personality to values stemming from their religious experience. All the great religious teachers have been conscious of the tension between good and evil or, to use Quaker terminology, between Light and Darkness in the world. Their prescriptions of how to deal with it have varied. Some have urged withdrawal into a life of prayer and meditation; others have enjoined us to do good works; many have insisted on unfailing belief in a God; and still others have recommended obedience to specific principles or rules of conduct. The life and teaching of Jesus includes all the prescriptions to some extent, but with obedience to rules of conduct having a low place on the list. What is more important, his life illustrates the fact that no man can escape the tension between good and evil either within himself or within the world. The whole point of Christ's message is missed if we overlook his personal struggle, as illustrated by the temptations in the wilderness, and his struggle with society, which culminated in the crucifixion. Both ended in a triumph for self-denial and

4

love. George Fox had similar experiences and, as with Jesus, his inner struggles had a social relevance.

Basic Quaker beliefs

The core of Quaker convictions consists of the recognition that life has its light and dark sides and the belief that all human beings are involved in the struggle to perceive and live according to the Light which will triumph over Darkness. Friends insist that with God's help and guidance everyone can find his own way towards the Light and that the discovery is made in his heart where it shines. Of course, he may be helped also by the study of the Bible or other religious books, by the example and teachings of others and by social experience.

A summary of Quaker beliefs in a few sentences would be grossly misleading if it omitted two elements of utmost importance to any understanding of their origins. One was the rejection of the doctrine of man's natural depravity which could only be redeemed by the external intervention of God, a doctrine central to orthodox Christianity. For Friends, the Light of Christ shone in the hearts of all men if only they would turn to it. The experience of Darkness was real enough to them but their faith was joyous and optimistic. They called themselves Children of the Light. Related to this was the other crucial element: A spontaneity and rebelliousness in the face of weighty learning and institutions. All their efforts were bent on assuring the free movement of the spirit.

The mysticism and child-like enthusiasm of Fox and other early Friends make it peculiarly difficult to communicate their experience in purely intellectual terms. However, the attempt has to be made and the first and most brilliant was by Robert Barclay in his *Apology*. To make Quaker beliefs intellectually acceptable, he formulated them in the context of contemporary theology and in the process of constructing a logical system he

5

lost some of the basic spontaneity of Friends. It has been said that while Barclay reinterpreted protestant orthodoxy according to a particular conception of the Inner Light, other Quaker writers of the late seventeenth century tended to reinterpret the insight of early Friends according to traditional protestant doctrine. All this may have been inevitable, but its effect was to give the world and the Society an impression of Quaker faith without some of its original flavour.[2]

The founders of the Quaker movement had tried to revive primitive Christianity. They were well versed in the Bible, the only record available for learning about Jesus and his disciples and the religious tradition from which they came, but they knew intuitively what Biblical scholarship has since confirmed. The record could not be regarded as wholly trustworthy by itself. Any attempt to convey religious experience distorts it to some extent through the process of communication. We cannot, therefore, rely entirely on the written or spoken word. No religious experience is valid unless it is confirmed in the ground of one's being.

The origins of the Peace Testimony can only be understood when we recall that George Fox and his followers sought to turn all men to the Light of Christ in their hearts and thus to transform the world. In this task, the weapons were spiritual and the use of military force of any kind was irrelevant and blasphemous, for it went clean contrary to the spirit of Christ. But it was a war nonetheless and occasionally some Friends confused the carnal and spiritual swords in their fervour.[3]

Friends called their struggle the Lamb's War, taking their text from *Revelation*, xvii, 14. It was war of a different kind and was graphically described by John Crook after the Peace of Ryswick in 1697:

> The end of the bloody or Lion's war must be the beginning of the Lamb's, who shall have the victory, not

6

by garments rolled in blood—for He wars not to destroy men's lives, but their corruptions and lusts, and to save their souls . . . and of the increase of His government and peace there shall be no end; for the stability of His times shall be righteousness and peace.[4]

The principal enemies against which men had to contend were their own pride and self-will. The triumph of Christ in the hearts of men was expected to affect their social relationships, but this was considered to be a natural consequence, as was the denial of military force. In a world transformed by Christ war simply had no place.[5]

What has come to be called the Peace Testimony was therefore a witness against war and all fightings with outward weapons, but not a witness against conflict between good and evil—far from it. Early Friends were involved in a great struggle in their hearts and in the world. They believed that the Kingdom of Christ could be realized there and then. The failure of their missionary enterprise led to a major change in outlook and method, but it did not weaken their conviction that Christian love overcomes all evil. Later generations of Friends pursued the struggle on more limited fronts.

The testimony against war in perspective

The history of the testimony against war is important not because it tells us what we should do today, but because it offers us a perspective of its place in the total Quaker witness. There is a fairly widespread view among Friends that if we could only recapture the spirit and mood of our founding fathers, we should regain some of the lost vigour of the Society. I do not think it can be done. The world today does not resemble seventeenth-century England. We are separated from the Founder of the Quaker movement by three centuries of change

7

and experience, and we should take very seriously the warning that:

> Quaker groups today need special caution against seeing early Friends in terms of modern religious experience. Early Quaker customs and Testimonies did not have the same meaning then that they have today, even where outward expression remains the same ... Modern liberal Quakers, for example, make liberals of their ancestors.[6]

The historical perspective does remind us of a number of fundamental points. First, the Quaker witness against war cannot be understood apart from the spiritual roots of Quakerism. Separate it from those roots and it will either wither and die for lack of nourishment or become stunted and deformed, exhibiting the worst superficialities of pacifism.

Secondly, because the attitude to war is rooted in a living faith it is a mixture of vision and realistic understanding of the world. The vision of the Kingdom of Christ on earth has not changed basically, but our understanding of the world has changed substantially with the accumulation of knowledge and experience.

In every generation Friends have been found among the visionaries and the realists, or, if you will, among the prophets and the reconcilers, according to which side their experience and personalities incline them. In speaking of someone as a 'visionary' or 'prophet', I stress that the person is filled by a vision of the ideal and attentive to its fulfilment. In calling someone a 'realist' or 'reconciler', I am emphasizing that his attention is focused on concrete particulars.

It does not follow that those strong in knowledge and understanding are to be found only among the realists and that those who are not must be visionaries. It could be just as well the other way round. A great Quaker scientist may have a profound knowledge and understanding of the physical universe, but be a complete idealist and show little appreciation of the complexities and confusions when venturing into the field of international politics. On the other hand, a Friend who has had little formal education and may not be exceptionally gifted in the scientific field can bring great wisdom to the affairs of men and be extremely effective in handling them, promoting those changes which improve the world a little.

Our personalities are probably more decisive as to which side we find ourselves on. We all have something of the visionary and realist in us, but in most the one outweighs the other. Only a rare few seem to combine both and achieve a triumphant witness which is a beacon to those who come after. Jeremiah and John Woolman were both visionaries and realists.

I speak with some feeling in this matter because I have always resented being placed in one or other category with the implication that I am a rather inferior specimen of a Quaker. Thinking about all those who have influenced me most, I note that it was precisely because one or other of these qualities was particularly strong in them. I have been much impressed by the caution and realism of some of my teachers at school and university, and some of my colleagues in Quaker international work. They have taught me the complexities and subtleties of the affairs of men and the limits of the individual. But their natural conservatism and pragmatism also made them tolerant, kindly and humble. I have also been strongly attracted by men and women, in and outside the Society, who have been true visionaries, dedicating their lives to one cause or another almost to the exclusion of all else. Their vigour, enthusiasm and combativeness have been tempered by generosity, genuineness and gaiety. I would not have done without the influence of either. In short, to be a healthy and vigorous Society we need both and the tension between them, but not their ordering in merit.

9

2

There is a third and most important point which arises when we place the testimony against war in its perspective. Because of their personal experience and convictions, Friends did not deny the reality of evil and of conflict. Nor did they equate conflict with evil.

They were well aware of the suffering which a non-violent witness could bring in an imperfect world. This is in contrast to those who identify peace with the absence of conflict and value that above all things. It is the latter who have given modern pacifism its bad name and have led their critics to refer to them contemptuously as 'passivists'. The failure to take evil and conflict into account as elements in our human condition and an obsession with the need for peace and harmony have led pacifists badly astray.

The inter-war period provides good examples of a position which amounted to advocating peace at any price. During the Czech crisis of 1938, some pacifists worried only about the danger of war. One of them wrote:

> A realistic view of the facts reveals the utter madness of another war to save Czechoslovakia, democracy, civilization or anything else worth saving.[7]

Christian pacifists were not exempt from the temptation to sacrifice others for the sake of peace. A commentary appearing in the organ of the Fellowship of Reconciliation at the same time, included the following statement:

> To make the appalling sacrifice of all justice and morality in recourse to war in order to avoid the comparatively small sacrifice of breaking up Czechoslovakia is a wicked absurdity.[8]

Excessive concentration on the evil and horror of war led not only to wishful thinking of the kind which ignored the true character of Hitler and his regime, but also to contradictions. Pacifists were to the fore among those who attacked imperialism and the economic exploitation of other peoples by the rich European powers. Hence, they consistently championed the nationalist movements in Asia and Africa. However, when there was a threat of war in Europe, the fate of the colonial people had to take second place:

> Would it help him (Hitler) to be reasonable in Czecho-slovakia if the British Government, which has threatened him if he advances in Czechoslovakia, uses the present moment to offer him an Empire settlement and an 'equal access to raw materials' such as Sir Samuel Hoare offered at Geneva in 1935?[9]

The implications of handing over subject peoples to exploitation by a brutal and racialist regime do not appear to have been considered.

It does not necessarily follow that one can draw a clear dividing line between religiously motivated pacifists with a profound insight into the moral dilemmas of the crisis and non-religious pacifists who slurred over the moral issues. The quotation from *Reconciliation* points to the weakness of a Christian pacifism when pacifism becomes a more important ingredient than Christianity. On the other hand, a secular body like the Women's International League for Peace and Freedom (British Section) urged the Government not to yield to German pressure, adding 'War may be postponed but cannot thus be averted.'

By and large, however, the comparative sanity of religious pacifist writing and propaganda sprang from the fact that pacifism was an outward expression of a faith which was a way of life and not just a philosophy. It will always remain a disputed question whether the teaching of Jesus was 'pacifist' or not; it is certain that those who seek to be his disciples will try to lead lives in which hatred and violence shall have no place. Christian pacifists of all denominations were unswerving in

11

their denunciation of war and the use of force as arbiters in international relations. They could not escape the temper of the times and were therefore preoccupied with disarmament and appeasement. However, in their writings they discussed the consequences of a policy of genuine non-violence, aware that it involved risks, sacrifices and suffering for those who chose such a way.

Changing concepts of 'peace'

In its essence, Friends' testimony against war was a concomitant of the struggle to realise the Kingdom of God on earth with spiritual weapons designed to conquer the evil in men's hearts and not to destroy their bodies or material possessions. It is well stated in the celebrated Declaration presented to King Charles II on 21 January, 1660–61. Quakers had a vision of what they meant by the establishment of Christ's Kingdom on earth:

> ... we do earnestly desire and wait, that (by the Word of God's Power, and its effectual operation in the hearts of men) the Kingdoms of this World may become the Kingdoms of the Lord, and of his Christ; that he might rule and reign in men by his spirit and truth; that thereby all people out of all different judgements and professions might be brought into love and unity with God, and one with another and that they might all come to witness the Prophets' words, who said 'Nation shall not lift up Sword against Nation, neither shall they learn war any more' (*Isaiah*, ii, 4, *Micah*, iv, 3).

From this they drew their principles of conduct:

> Our principle is, and our practices have always been, to seek peace and ensue it, and to follow after righteousness and the knowledge of God, seeking the good and welfare,

and doing that which tends to the peace of All. . . . The Spirit of Christ, by which we are guided, is not changeable, so as once to command us from a thing as evil, and again to move unto it; and we do certainly know, and do testify to the world, that the Spirit of Christ which leads us into all Truth, will never move us to fight and war against any man with outward weapons, neither for the Kingdom of Christ, nor for the kingdoms of this world.[10]

Their attitude to war was essentially negative.[11] Friends had nothing to say about the art of government and how wars might be avoided in an unconverted world. They realised that it would remain imperfect until their work was done, which accounts for their apparently ambiguous statements about accepting institutions based upon the ultimate sanction of armed force. Indeed, George Fox advised Friends to pay taxes to the government whose duty it was to keep the peace.[12]

After the first flush of enthusiasm, the Society became settled and organized. Yet, although it was resigned to existing in an imperfect world, the idea of peace remained vague and Friends did not feel called upon to advocate any specific measures which would reduce the incidence of war, other than to remind each other to live peaceably. There were good historical reasons for this, as we shall see.

I have not been very successful in an attempt to discover when Friends first formally referred to their testimony against bearing arms and fighting as The Peace Testimony. It is, however, interesting to note that in the 1883 edition of the Book of Discipline, the section which refers to this testimony is headed 'Testimony on War', whereas it has become 'Peace among Nations' after the next revision in 1911, thus indicating a greater concern with the institutional aspects of international relations. When the word 'peace' was used in official documents of the Society in the mid-eighteenth century, the emphasis was directed towards the personal conduct of Friends. For example:

> ... it behoveth us to hold forth the ensign of the Lamb of God, and, by our patience and peaceable behaviour, to shew that we walk in obedience to the example and precepts of our Lord and Master, who hath commanded to love our enemies, and do good even to them that hate us. Wherefore we intreat all who profess themselves members of our society, to be faithful to that ancient testimony, borne by us ever since we were a people, against bearing arms and fighting, that by a conduct agreeable to our profession, we may demonstrate ourselves to be real followers of the Messiah, the peaceable Saviour, of the increase of whose government and peace there shall be no end.[13]

Peace was not primarily a political concept but one of personal behaviour. Friends were given negative advice: Not to join the militia, not to arm ships, not to make profit out of war. They were called upon to be meek, humble and peaceful in their bearing. At the height of the Napoleonic Wars, Yearly Meeting came to the following conclusion:

> On the calamitous subject of war, we do not feel much now to say. Friends, you are not ignorant of what adorns our profession, with respect to this subject. Only this would we say, make it not a topic of conversation. Guard against placing your dependence on fleets and armies; be peaceable yourselves, in words and actions; and pray to the father of the universe that He would breathe the spirit of reconciliation into the hearts of his erring and contending creatures.[14]

Nevertheless, a political concept was not entirely absent and was sometimes hinted at through Biblical references. The personal witness had to lead to social consequences if it was to have any meaning. So the hope was frequently expressed that others would be influenced by the Quaker example:

> Most, if not all, people admit the transcendent excellency of peace . . . Some people then must begin to fulfil the evangelical promise, and cease to learn war any more . . . Friends, it is an awful thing to stand forth to the nation as the advocates of inviolable peace; and our testimony loses its efficacy in proportion to the want of consistency in any.[15]

By the mid-nineteenth century, Friends had gone further. They related their testimony to a pressing political problem and referred to a specific procedure for resolving conflict. London Yearly Meeting Epistle of 1846 commented on threatened hostilities with the United States in the following words:

> Our testimony against all wars and fightings is truly a Christian testimony . . . We hail, . . ., many instances of later years, in which disputes between nations have been settled by arbitration, and not by a recourse to the anti-Christian practice of war.[16]

The sources of authority

In the course of its historical evolution, Friends' stand against war acquired a personal as well as a social and political aspect, but the personal basis came first. Whatever we do, we are conscious of the struggle and tension within our hearts. In society, we seek to create the opportunity for each member to make his contribution and thus fulfil himself in the service of God. The experience of Friends confirms the beautiful words of the Second Collect, for peace, in *The Book of Common Prayer* of the Church of England:

> O God, who art the author of peace and lover of concord, in knowledge of whom standeth our eternal life, whose service is perfect freedom . . .

This may seem a simple, optimistic and naive faith in our sophisticated and scientific age. It has left its distinctive mark on the expression that Friends give to their testimonies. They regard human problems as being essentially religious and lay stress on the spiritual, moral and psychological factors involved in any human situation. The emphasis on personal action, which in the case of war means abstention, inevitably raises the problem of where one draws the line. In the total wars of the first half of this century, Quakers accepted non-combatant service with the armed forces, served in an independent but uniformed Friends Ambulance Unit, relieved the sufferings of civilian war victims, did alternative civilian service of 'national importance' at home, went to prison for refusing any service which might assist the war effort, even fire-watching. Some refused to pay taxes.

There are no formal rules laid down for Quaker conduct in such circumstances, other than to follow the Light of Christ. In an earlier age, John Woolman described what this meant for the individual over the issue of paying war tax:

> I was told that Friends in England frequently paid taxes, when the money was applied to such purposes. I had conference with several noted Friends on the subject, who all favoured the payment of such taxes, some of whom I preferred before myself, and this made me easier for a time. Yet there was in the deeps of my mind a scruple which I never could get over, and at certain times I was greatly distressed on that account.

> I all along believed that there were some upright-hearted men, who paid such taxes, but could not see that their example was a sufficient reason for me to do so, . . .[17]

The absence of an authoritarian or hierarchical structure in their religion gives Quakers some undoubted advantages in dealing with contemporary problems. The Society of Friends has always been a 'participatory democracy', which has been described as the only positive political slogan of the revolutionary wave which hit the Western World in the late 1960s.[18]

Fox certainly did not have in mind 'participatory democracy' in the contemporary sense, when he set up Monthly and Quarterly Meetings. He saw the business meeting as under the authority and power of God. The sole object was to discover the Will of God in dealing with any situation or problem. Hence, the Quaker business meeting is also a meeting for worship. Every member has something to contribute to the common search, whether in silence or through the spoken word.

Friends have their full measure of human foibles and those familiar with Quaker business meetings know only too well how imperfect they can be—the sheer boredom of it all. The Quaker brand of 'participatory democracy' creaks and groans, it can get bogged down in trivia, and the need for a unity of minds can result in procrastinations and inaction. Yet, in spite of all, it works. Where 'participatory democracy' has so often meant talk and no action, Friends have made it effective through their insistence on the responsibility of the individual from which he cannot escape by blaming the majority, or the minority; or by indulging in the current fashion for *self*-fulfilment and doing *one's own* thing. A failure in business meeting, or in meeting for worship, cannot be attributed to 'them'. From such a meeting, each one goes away asking himself 'where have I failed in my responsibilities?'

Friends also sit lightly to doctrine and ideologies and this is a special advantage in our times. By their profession they should not be tied to 'isms or institutions. In practice it is extraordinarily difficult not to be so tied. There are some, for instance, who are wedded to pacifism above all else and others to whom the committee becomes more important than its

17

business. On the whole, however, Friends are sensitive to the changing environment in which they live and to new insights into the condition of man. This has the corollary that they should be ready constantly to challenge and test established authority of all kinds, including that of their own historical tradition. However, they also have their share of human conservatism so that ideas and practices begin to acquire a life of their own. Hence, there is a danger that the witness about war and peace becomes institutionalized, meaning that it is tied to a particular analysis of the world, which may have added to insight and understanding at the time when it arose, but that has lost some of its relevance in subsequent ages in the light of new experiences.

To take an example near our time: People in the nineteenth century were filled with the idea of the inevitability of human progress. All that was needed was the right frame of mind, the right methods and the right institutions, and mankind would march forward steadily to the golden age. They had made the important discovery that psychology and institutions are major factors in determining the causes of war, but their optimism makes strange reading in the light of the events since the First World War. In 1910, John William Graham wrote in *The Friend*, asking 'Are the times ripe for Peace?' He answered that outward circumstances indicated it and that only an outdated psychology prevented it:

> It looks as though the psychological attitude of military expectancy and fear was surviving after the need for it had passed.[19]

Change the psychology and you are assured of peace. We know today that the problems of war and peace are far too complex to be dealt with on one level alone. That is why it is insufficient to go about the world quoting Fox and early Friends as the answer to its problems.

18

Looking at it from another angle, we find that the historical context will dictate to a large extent the expression of our testimony against war. Since groups and institutions are slow to adapt to changing circumstances, there is a natural tendency to stand fast and to defend what has become a hallowed expression of one's view. The reverse of this is not to abandon all that has been handed down through the generations. The experience of early Friends contained an element of the Truth that is no less real today than it was three hundred and twenty years ago.

In his *Christian Pacifism in History*,[20] Geoffrey Nuttall reviews the Christian pacifist position in different periods and concludes that:

> each successive group, whether consciously or not, built on the foundations laid, or the substructure left, by those who had gone before, accepting earlier perceptions or arguments and adding something of their own . . .

It has been the same in the history of the Quaker witness against war, which is the subject of the next chapter.

II

THE PEACE TESTIMONY IN HISTORY

The historical development of the Society of Friends has been influenced by the social and political climate of the times. Different aspects and different problems of the Quaker faith have been stressed in different ages. But through it runs a constant opposition to all war and fighting, and a belief that true progress is only achieved through the power of Christian love. If we place the Society's history in its social and political context, we may revise our estimate of the importance and significance of some Quaker thought and activities, but that does not necessarily involve a repudiation of the basic Quaker message.

At least six distinct historical periods provide the background for a study of Friends' testimony against war. The first covers the two decades until about 1670. Then follows the century which ends in 1776. The third period marks the revolutionary age until about 1815, after which comes the age of nineteenth-century optimism, ending abruptly in 1914, which is followed by the era of total war. The sixth and contemporary period may be said to have begun in 1945.

Such classifications are bound to seem arbitrary. They recall the problem of deciding when the Middle Ages began and when they ended. Be that as it may, I have made the divisions because in each period major developments outside and within the Society gave a distinct colouring to its stand over the issues of war and peace.

The birth of the Quaker movement

The Quaker movement was born amidst religious and political ferment which was a consequence of the economic and social upheavals of the seventeenth century. All forms of authority were under attack. Intolerance and violence were the order of the day. The founders of the Society of Friends had been through the Civil Wars. A substantial number of early Quakers, including some of their outstanding leaders, had served in the armies and navies of both sides. That experience may well explain their fighting spirit and their fervent renunciation of outward weapons.

The struggle in England was between King and Parliament for control over the state, ultimately culminating in the triumph of Parliament. Beneath the political and constitutional issues lay the confrontation of social, economic and religious forces. In the military sphere, the conflict posed the problem of reconciling armed force as the prerogative of the sovereign with the rights of the subject over taxation and his personal freedom. The milestones in the struggle: The Petition of Right (1628); Parliament's demand for control of the militia and fortified places (1641–42); The Declaration of Right (1689); are well known.

It is significant that the Quaker movement began in a period when the army controlled civil government. This presented early Friends with a dilemma. Although their spiritual ancestry may be traced back to the mystical tradition in Christianity, they owed a great deal to Puritanism and were part of the Puritan movement. They were therefore more at home in the religious climate of Cromwellian England than in that of Stuart England. Yet, the social background of the movement among the sturdy and independent farming folk, particularly weavers, in the rural areas, and the skilled artisans, particularly tailors and leather workers, of the towns, brought it into conflict with the social and economic interests of the classes on the side of the Puritan revolution. In short, Quakerism:

> derived its main support from precisely those sections of the population which found their economic position threatened and their political demands frustrated by the political and social upheavals of the seventeenth century.[21]

This background helps to explain the fiercely independent and personal stand of early Friends.

Warfare in the seventeenth century was an affair of small armies. Weapons and logistics were at a stage which prevented military operations from being a highly organized or consistent activity. Nonetheless, because of the revolutionary situation in the country, every individual was involved in the great conflicts of the age. It meant that while Friends were opposed to war, they were caught up in what a Quaker historian has described as a 'deadlock of consciences'[22]—a situation in which ideals were irreconcilably antagonistic. There was no question of withdrawing and standing to one side, letting the battle rage around them.

This involvement, combined with their denial of fighting with outward weapons, established the two principal aspects of what we now call the Peace Testimony. One was negative: The refusal to take up arms. The other was positive: The commitment to the triumph of the spirit of Christ in the hearts of all men. Neither can exist without the other, although they have not always been equally stressed at different times in the subsequent history of the Society. They were rooted in a prophetic religion.

Organization and 'Quietism'

Within two decades of their emergence as a movement, Friends' vision of sweeping all before them into the Light began to evaporate. The political effects of the Restoration of 1660 and the severe persecution of dissenters forced them to organize and to establish their 'harmlessness' in the eyes of authority, so as to assure their survival.

In becoming organized, Friends acquired many of the attributes of a religious sect, which George Fox had declared they were not. Among them were withdrawal from the world's corruption and sin; insistence on obedience to their ethic in every detail; expectation of remaining a minority; fixed delimitation of membership. But they retained sufficient of the openness of their founders to regard their principles as having universal relevance. This became a source of power from which they derived the strength to deal with the needs and problems of the world at large. Nor did they turn their religious beliefs into a new creed. Friends held fast to the vision that 'The Spirit moved and drew men together, but there was no limit to where it might reach.'[23]

They had to work hard to establish their innocence before the government. During the Restoration crisis some Quakers had become involved in resistance to the Royalists, some were even named as national commissioners of the militia. Fox's first reaction was confused, but later he reaffirmed the Quaker refusal to use any but spiritual weapons.

In 1661, Friends had fallen under suspicion of being implicated in the rising of the Fifth Monarchy Men. They used their testimony against war and fighting as proof that they could be trusted not to rebel or plot revolution. The famous Declaration of that time, to which I have referred in the previous chapter, also served as a public relations exercise. It was widely diffused and pointedly directed against 'Plotters', as well as 'Fighters'. In it the Government was urged 'not to wrong the innocent'.

Henceforth, reiterations of that testimony combined a rehearsal of the reasons why Friends originally took this stand, with assurances that the Society did not wish to interfere in the affairs of state. When the discovery of a Jacobite plot to murder William III led to the establishment of an 'Association' to swear loyalty to the King and to offer him armed protection, Meeting for Sufferings ordered the presentation of a paper which expressed the position of Friends as follows:

> The setting up and putting down Kings and Governments is God's peculiar prerogative, for causes best known to himself, and that it is not our work and business to have any hand or continuance therein, nor to be busybodies in matters above our station . . . And whereas we, the said people, are required to sign the said Association, we sincerely declare that our refusing to do so is not out of any disaffection to the King or Government, nor in opposition to his being declared rightful and lawful King of these realms, but purely because we cannot for conscience' sake fight, kill, or revenge either for ourselves or any man else.[24]

Nevertheless, protestations of neutrality in political disputes did not save them from suffering, as they learnt to their cost during Monmouth's rebellion in 1685 and the Revolution of 1688, when they fell under the suspicion of both sides.

As the Society settled down in the last quarter of the seventeenth century, the prophetic and humanitarian aspects of its attitude to war emerged side by side. The first was stressed by Robert Barclay, whose *Apology* contains an unequivocal denunciation of war on the basis of the Scriptures. His address to the plenipotentiaries negotiating the Treaty of Nimeguen in 1678, prophesied that it would be no more than an armed truce unless it was governed by Christian principles. It also affirmed that those who were governed by the divine Light and suffered like Jesus would overcome. He prefaced his remarks with

3

becoming humility and firmness. He knew that he would be considered weak, foolish and unworldly. He respected authority but he had to intervene on behalf of Christ, whose

> authority has been contemned, his laws broken, his Life oppressed, his standard of peace pulled down and rent, his Government encroached upon: What shall I say, his precious blood shed, and himself afresh crucified, and put to open shame by the murders and cruelties that have attended those wars.[25]

Barclay's words are an interesting mixture. The intercession on behalf of Christ has the same fire that distinguished the utterances of Fox and his followers, but the references to his hesitations before speaking out betray some resignation to the existence of an imperfect world.

The second aspect was represented in Penn's *Essay Towards the Present and Future Peace of Europe*, whose relevance to our times was discussed by Duncan Wood in the Swarthmore Lecture of 1962.[26] Although this effort at practical peace-making sprang from his religious experience and convictions, Penn makes an appeal which could have been made by the utilitarian philosophers of the nineteenth century:

> What can we desire better than Peace, but the Grace to use it? Peace preserves our possessions; we are in no danger of invasions; our trade is free and safe; and we rise and lie down without anxiety. The rich bring out their hoards, and employ the poor manufactors; buildings and divers projections for profit and pleasure, go on: it excites industry, which brings wealth, as that gives the means of charity and hospitality, not the lowest ornaments of a kingdom or commonwealth. But war, like the frost of 83, seizes all these comforts at once, and stops the civil channels of society. The rich draw in their stock, the poor

turn soldiers, or thieve, or starve; no industry, no building, no manufactury, little hospitality or charity; but what the peace gave, the war devours.[27]

With his *Essay* and the 'Holy Experiment' in Pennsylvania, Penn launched a long series of Quaker endeavours—by individuals and groups—to make a practical contribution to peace in an imperfect world. He established the humanitarian tradition in the work of Friends.

The beginning of the eighteenth century thus saw the emergence of the Peace Testimony as we have come to think of it. At its centre was the conviction that war was contrary to the spirit of Christ. After the failure to transform the world, Friends concentrated on preserving the purity of their vision and behaved like a faithful remnant which must keep the flame alight in its midst. With Penn there began the practice of working for improvements which would help men to live in peace until the world was transformed.

Two other characteristics also made their appearance at this time. Partly because of their philosophy of life and partly as the result of their sufferings under various persecutions, Friends were sensitive to the sufferings of others and did everything they could to relieve them. This applied particularly to the victims of war. Secondly, because of the unsettled state of English society in the late seventeenth century, Friends were much preoccupied with the problem of rebellion and were emphatic in their opposition to armed insurrection of any kind. For instance, the only reference to the security of Pennsylvania in Penn's 'Frame of Government' made provision against subversion but contained no mention of the threat of war.

All these developments reflected the transitory nature of the times. Nevertheless, despite periodic outbreaks of fanaticism and persecution, the last decades of the century in England were marked by a growing tolerance, a decline in religious fervour, and increasing social and political order. There were plenty of wars, but they were fought outside the country, if we exclude Ireland.

Military technology was now sufficiently advanced to make warfare more bloody and destructive. This had the triple effect of inspiring caution in some—but by no means all—commanders, of giving them the possibility of greater control over operations and of providing the opportunity to be more precise in defining their objectives.

The commanders, too, were changing. The mercenary officer of the seventeenth century was giving way to the aristocratic officer. The absolute rulers of Europe required a permanent force led by the nobility of the realm, whose claim to leadership was based on birth and wealth and who were held to have a natural genius for command.

War became stylised. The marching season lasted a few months and for the rest of the year armies retired to winter quarters. Often a campaign culminated in one battle, provided the armies could find each other. The battle itself followed certain rituals and this was not surprising in an age where the officers of the contending forces had more in common with each other than with their own soldiers. For most Englishmen such conflicts were quite remote as the Hanoverian kings relied on German mercenaries to do their fighting on the Continent and in the colonies.

Around 1720, the Society entered upon a period of Quietism in England. Its main activities during the 'quiet' period focused on worship and maintaining discipline among its members in conformity with the traditional testimonies. The problem of social reform was not wholly neglected but left to the initiative of individuals.

Quakers, as nonconformists, were excluded from official positions and were mainly engaged in commercial and industrial pursuits. However, they could not escape completely from the challenge and temptations arising from war. In the naval sphere there were problems of conscience over the arming of ships against privateers, letters of marque,* the activities of press gangs and the trade in arms. At home, Friends were faced with the call to service in the militia and those who did not take an absolute stand were tempted to buy their way out of the obligation by providing money for a substitute. Quaker records of this time are full of concern for members who either betrayed the testimony against war, or were forced against their will to become soldiers or sailors, or suffered loss of property for their refusal to cooperate.

By and large, the Society was little disturbed by the state of the country. Indeed, it was most unhappy at the prospect of any sudden change which threatened its members' peace of mind and profits. In 1746, Yearly Meeting forgot itself and presented a most fulsome address to George II, congratulating him on the defeat of the Jacobite Rebellion. Generally, however, Friends tried to be faithful to their testimony against war, only there seemed little bite in repeated statements to that effect.

American Quakers also passed through Quietism, but at a later time because the practical experiments of government in Pennsylvania, New Jersey and Rhode Island had kept them very much involved with the world. Moreover, the wars with the French and their Indian allies, and the Revolution of 1776, gave little respite to Friends on the subject of peace and war.

The age of revolutionary wars, 1776–1815
The apparently well-ordered world of the eighteenth century was shattered by a succession of revolutionary wars which began in America and then spread to Europe. Armies were no

* A royal licence to fit out an armed vessel (privateer) and use it for the capture of enemy merchant ships.

longer the instruments of absolute, even if enlightened, rulers. The American colonies fought for their freedom with a citizen army. The French Revolution spread its democratic message across the Continent with mass armies. Their impact on the rest of Europe laid the foundations of modern military organization.

There were several reasons for this development. At its root lay the modern nation state which had its origins in the absolute monarchies of the seventeenth and eighteenth centuries. In due course, competitive nationalisms replaced dynastic rivalries. France set the pattern and Prussia was the first to follow suit. The ideology of nationalism was associated with democracy and freedom. In practice, it led easily to authoritarian rule and imperialism.

With nationalism came the concept of the 'nation in arms'. The conflict between the aristocracy and the middle classes for control over military affairs, which had accompanied the rise of nationalism, was mirrored in the armed forces by a shift from the amateur to the professional among the officers and from the mercenary and the impressed poor to the citizen soldier among the rank and file.

These developments seemed far removed from the concerns of British and American Quakers. Britain stood largely outside the mainstream of the changes. This was partly because it had had its 'revolution' one hundred and fifty years earlier when the issue of who was to control the armed forces of the state was decided; and partly because Britain had no direct experience of warfare with mass armies. Thus British Friends saw the challenge of war in the form to which they had long been accustomed: Militia duty; the press-ganging of young men; the arming of ships; dealing in prize goods, etc.

American Friends were brought face to face with the realities of revolutionary war in 1776. Some members put their patriotic duties before their religious principles and were duly excluded from the Society. One of them, Nathaniel Greene, became a distinguished commander of the revolutionary army; a good illustration that membership of the Society of Friends does not imply a lack of martial gifts. However, the official response of the Society conformed to the practices of a religious sect bent on preserving the purity of its spiritual vocation. Friends in Pennsylvania opposed the dissolution of the union with England by Congress. Meeting for Sufferings in Philadelphia proclaimed its loyalty to the established government. During the hostilities Friends were neutral and relieved suffering, regardless of who was the victim. They also opposed the revolution on grounds which were made clear in a memorable exchange between George Washington and Warner Mifflin,* after the United States had won their independence:

Washington: Mr. Mifflin, will you please to inform me on what principles you were opposed to the Revolution?

Mifflin: Yes, friend Washington; upon the same principles that I should be opposed to a change in this government. All that ever was gained by revolutions, are not an adequate compensation to the poor mangled soldier, for the loss of life or limb.

Washington: Mr. Mifflin, I honour your sentiments;—there is more in that than mankind have generally considered.[28]

The full brunt of the horrors of war in this period was experienced by Friends in Ireland during the rebellion of 1798. They were caught between two sides who waged a conflict of the utmost savagery, and their conduct became the epitome of the Peace Testimony in action: Absolute non-participation in

---

* Warner Mifflin (1745–1798): Prominent American Friend and pioneer of the anti-slavery movement. During the War of Independence he travelled at great personal risk across the lines to put the Quaker view to the American and English commanders, Washington and Howe.

the struggle; refusal to provide themselves with any means of self-defence; relief of suffering and the provision of refuge to people on both sides; readiness to suffer insults and physical assault. They were open in their dealings with all parties and displayed great moral and physical courage.

Generally speaking, the Society was not sufficiently affected by the great wars at the turn of the century to be moved to do more than watch carefully over the faithfulness of its members in upholding traditional testimonies. Individual Friends were more aware of the times and stand out from an essentially inward-turned sect. In their concerns they combined the universalism of early Friends with the rational humanitarianism of the eighteenth century. John Woolman and Anthony Benezet in America, Elizabeth Fry and William Tuke in England, are outstanding examples in the field of social reform. Others played a prominent part in the establishment and activities of peace societies at the end of the Napoleonic Wars.

The nineteenth century

The changes produced by the age of revolutionary warfare worked themselves out in Europe during the decades after 1815. Among them were technological innovations which had an important bearing on the development of the modern army. Two, in particular, must be mentioned: The invention of new weapons and their diversification, and the introduction of railways.

Weapons increased in destructive power. They required skilled handling and careful integration with other weapons. Their effect was to promote functional specialization. Railways speeded up the movement of large masses of men, greatly extended the range of warfare and required complex organization. Their effect was to promote systematic strategic planning and the organization of staff work.

The officer's job had become full-time and could no longer be combined with looking after one's estates, local government duties or attendance at the court. The emergence of a distinct military profession was accompanied by the formulation of an ethos which defined the soldier's relationship to society, his duties to the state and, in a less explicit way, represented a particular *Weltanschauung* or philosophy.

Higher institutions for the study of military affairs and the organization of general staffs promoted the military ethos through the socialization of the officers. Both, incidentally, had their origins in Prussia where Scharnhorst founded the Kriegsakademie in 1810, for a long time to remain the only institution of its kind. The general staff did not come into existence until after 1850. By the mid-nineteenth century, about half the world's literature on military affairs was published in Germany, including the great study by Clausewitz. War had become a science.

The full impact of all these developments burst upon the world in the series of armed confrontations which began with the American Civil War (1861–65). It was the first total war of modern times because of the extent to which it involved the whole population and of the ravages it caused. American Friends were again exposed to the horrors of war, but this time they were caught in a dilemma which has a particular relevance to our times.

Many Friends had struggled arduously for the emancipation of slaves. They, particularly the younger members, were torn between what seemed to be the noblest cause of their time and their loyalty to the anti-war testimony of the Society. A number volunteered for the Unionist army. The Society as a body stood by its historic position.

With the introduction of the draft, all Friends were challenged directly and the younger men of military age had to make a choice. In the North, the climate of opinion was not too hostile on account of the general unpopularity of conscription and the personal sympathy of Abraham Lincoln for Friends. In the South, Quakers suffered grievously but did not experience the inner conflict as acutely, as there was little doubt where their sympathies lay over the issue of the war. Most of them supported the abolitionist cause.[29]

After the Civil War, Friends organized a Peace Conference at Baltimore in 1866. It was attended by representatives of the 'orthodox' yearly meetings in the United States, who reaffirmed the conviction that 'Peace is the necessary consequence of the full acceptance of the Gospel of our Lord and Saviour Jesus Christ'. American Friends were also deeply impressed by the cost of the war, which seemed too great a price to pay for even the noblest of causes. In these calculations they shared the concern of many English Friends.

England was only remotely affected by war for most of the nineteenth century. The one major conflict in which it was engaged was the war with Russia from 1854 to 1856. It was still essentially an eighteenth-century army which fought in the Crimea with such disastrous results. As a direct consequence there began the slow movement of reform which was eventually to bring the structure and management of the army into line with those of the great continental powers. However, its modernization was not completed until after the further *débâcle* against the Boers at the end of the century.

An army which was primarily an instrument for policing the Empire was remote from the people. Moreover, this was the age of optimism, based on the prosperity of the country, though by no means evenly shared among its citizens, and the ability of the navy to keep war at a distance. It is not surprising that Friends, who had become prosperous through the pursuit of trade and industry, should have come under the influence of liberal utilitarian thought whose analysis of war and its causes rested on the following argument.

War does not pay because it is destructive of the material well-being of the people, which is based on production and trade that can only flourish in peacetime. Therefore, peace is in everyone's interest. This is only rational, but why do states act irrationally? The answer is that governments find war a convenient excuse to raise taxes, to increase the power of the executive and thus to extend their control over the citizen. The solution is to change the nature of the state and its government, and that can only be done through the creation of an educated and informed democracy, because war is so obviously against the interests of the people.

Underlying this reasoning was the assumption that the state could be improved because men were rational. There would be disputes among states, just as there were disputes among men, but the propensity to resort to war would gradually disappear and be replaced by a tendency to settle international quarrels rationally and amicably, just as the rule of law, based on reason and consent, had come to prevail within the state. This sketch does not, of course, do justice to the detailed argument behind these conclusions nor to the variety and nuances of liberal thought. However, its basic assumptions had a wide appeal and John Bright was a prominent exponent of this kind of view among Friends.[30]

The optimistic philosophy about the nature of man and the state was expressed in Quaker writings and activities. The latter included participation in International Peace Congresses all over Europe, which provided platforms for the rehearsal of economic arguments against war and deliberated about the best means for the settlement of international disputes. It is an interesting fact that in an age of mass warfare, Friends and other workers for peace turned to mass action in their anti-war

35

propaganda. This was the case with the publication of the *Christian Appeal* in 1855. Two hundred and twenty thousand copies were distributed, including five thousand each in French and German.[31]

More important is the tenor of the *Christian Appeal*, which was directed against the Crimean War and urged the members of both Houses of Parliament to 'remember that that which is morally and religiously wrong cannot be politically right'. Whatever the currents of the time, Friends never quite forgot the source of their testimony against war. This stood out in the celebrated Quaker deputation to the Czar of Russia in the winter of 1854, with its unsuccessful attempt to forestall the impending conflict. The address to Nicholas I appealed to him to act as a Christian and did not 'offer any opinion on the questions now at issue.'[32]

Friends also gave expression to Christian love in the relief of Finland after the war and in the work of the Friends' War Victims Relief Fund during the Franco-Prussian War. Here again, the more war became organized on a large scale, the more the response of the Society was through the organization and institutionalization of its work. The appointment of standing Peace Committees by London Yearly Meeting in 1888 and by Philadelphia (Race Street) Yearly Meeting in 1892 were important steps in this direction.[33]

The response to total war, 1914–1945

The World Wars of this century introduced yet another dimension to warfare. They were total wars in the fullest sense of the word. Every man, woman and child was involved. The character of the conflict was not recognized at first. There was no provision for industrial mobilization in 1914 and it was only after the establishment of the stalemate on the Western Front and the fearful slaughter of trench warfare that it became necessary to mobilize the nation's resources and to gear the whole economy to the pursuit of war. In addition, the use of air forces helped to remove the distinction between the front line and the home base. Total warfare was accompanied by the emergence of totalitarian ideologies. Not since the seventeenth century had there been such pitiless strife for the triumph or defeat of some ideological system.

The traumatic impact of these events left their mark on the attitude of Friends. They did not lose sight of their basic religious message, but it is no exaggeration that the Peace Testimony was seen as the most important contribution which Friends had to offer to solving the problems of the world. Significantly, this widely shared concern was a major element in the process of healing the wounds caused by the schisms among American Friends. Different and even opposed yearly meetings found a ground for common action in support of the American Friends Service Committee.

The Peace Testimony became a vehicle for political action. Quakers threw their efforts and enthusiasm into the struggle to prevent a repetition of the holocaust through disarmament, the promotion of economic justice and the construction of institutions to preserve peace. They tried to further international friendship through work camps and Quaker 'Embassies'. The latter were set up in cities which were focal points of international relations and tensions: Paris, Berlin, Warsaw, Geneva. After the Second World War, Friends' activities spread to the organization of international student seminars, and conferences for diplomats and other élite groups.

Not all Friends were equally conscious of the religious roots of their work. Among those who were, Carl Heath combined a keen awareness of what he was up against with the fundamental optimism of the spiritual reformer. He had conceived the idea of Quaker 'Embassies' and his own position was firmly grounded in his religious faith. At the end of the First World War he appealed to Friends:

> ... to use the great call and opportunity, which the return of peace will give to the Society to carry the message of the Universal Christ and the humane and democratic Spirit to every part of the new Europe that will arise out of the destruction of the old.[34]

During the Second World War he showed his understanding of the implications of the Quaker position when he disagreed with those Friends who were trying to find some way of stopping the war by public action. He wrote in 1941:

> It is unreal to reject the fact that peace-reaching (*sic*) needs a deep spiritual effort and widespread preparedness. Without these, all the demands to stop fighting amount to little. The war goes on, for the spirit that can command peace is not there.[35]

Yet, in effect, the witness of Friends had become secularized. Even Carl Heath linked the message of the Universal Christ to the 'democratic' spirit, implying a political concept, the meaning of which is much disputed.

Friends were also subject to the temptation of flattery and facile optimism. Quite naturally, they were pleased to be trusted and admired, and to be appreciated by Nazis and Communists because they offered 'neutral ground'. The belief that opponents might learn to understand and appreciate each other through dialogues in a friendly and relaxed atmosphere lay behind much of Quaker peace-work in the inter-war period. It was refined after 1945, when people were brought together for prolonged periods of study of international and world problems. The work camp movement went further and sought to promote international understanding and reconciliation through participation in some socially useful physical labour.

It is noteworthy that any conscious formulation of the Quaker message was avoided in these activities, on the perfectly reasonable ground that actions speak louder and more effectively than words. Moreover, in view of the fact that the participants came from different religious backgrounds and that many of them had no religious beliefs at all, it would have been doubly inappropriate to give them the impression that one was out to convert them to Quakerism. Inappropriate in an enterprise devoted to bringing together people of such different and opposing views with the aim of encouraging friendship and peace; inappropriate also because Friends have always resisted the implication that any particular organized form of religion is superior to any other.

I remember how the reluctance to push ourselves forward often led to very brief and heavily 'humanitarian' explanations of the Quaker background. We were a little ashamed of Fox; it was easier to put Woolman across. A thorough discussion of the motives behind these activities would only take place under pressure from the curious and puzzled participants. Even then, the explanation of the Quaker faith was muted and almost apologetic. After one of my attempts to explain Quakerism, a Dutch social scientist commented: 'Interesting; typical of Anglo-Saxon vagueness and lack of logic.'

In spite of the sponsors' reserve and hesitations, there were always some who were profoundly moved by these experiences, and one or two joined the Society. Small groups of Friends had also emerged again on the European Continent, directly as the result of Quaker work for the relief of suffering and for reconciliation. Thus the spirit broke through occasionally without much deliberate help from Friends.

Work in the field of internation relations had become the concern of the whole Society, but only a small proportion of its membership could be actively engaged in it. In one respect, however, total war did make Friends' testimony once more a personal problem for all. Conscription made conscientious objection an issue for the whole Society. Friends were reminded of their responsibilities and the old question of where to draw the line revived in the modern context. As in earlier periods, the Society's response was divided between proclaiming the message that lay behind the refusal to take up arms and practical concern for the relief of conscientious objectors, as well as the wish to prove the good citizenship of Friends.

Some lessons from the past

In our unhistorically-minded age it is a hazardous undertaking to try to point to the lessons of the past. A whole school of academic thinkers has arisen in the social sciences whose anxiety to prove that their approach is scientific has made them dismiss the value of the humanities, particularly history, as a study which might throw light on contemporary problems. They point out with considerable justice that reliance on the past as a guide often hinders understanding of the present. Nowhere has this been more true than in military affairs. Strategists and generals are inclined to prepare for the previous war. They embarked on the First World War on the assumption that it would be a fast-moving affair with a few decisive battles on the lines of the Franco-Prussian War forty years earlier. They, at least the British and French commanders, embarked on the Second World War expecting a long-protracted positional war of attrition. Only a few military thinkers had studied the development of new technologies and weapons and had tried to devise strategies and tactics to make use of them.

As a Society with more than three hundred years of history behind it, we cannot avoid meditating on the heritage of our past in order to gain an insight into our present condition.

There is another more important reason why Friends should ponder over their history. We believe that each one must experience the prompting of Christ in his own heart. However, that inner authority has to be tested repeatedly for it is easy to confuse with self-will. There are several ways in which experience can be tested and they are not mutually exclusive. It can be submitted to the examination of the group—the time-honoured method of dealing with concerns in the Society. It can be submitted to the light of teaching in the Bible and other religious literature. It can be compared with the individual and corporate experience of Friends. It is the last method that concerns us here. Earlier generations of Friends have lived in different circumstances and had different perceptions of the world, but that inner power which compelled them to live and act in the way they did is the same as the one we claim to be the source of our strength today.

When we stand back and look at the history of the Quaker Peace Testimony, we note that it cannot be separated from the events of the time. War was all around early Friends. They could not escape it. They were also passionately involved in the central debate of the age, which was couched in religious terms. After the first decades, Quakers organized themselves for survival and were gradually pushed on to the fringes of society. As a result, their message lost its spontaneity. For the next hundred years warfare became more restricted and was an intermittent experience for some groups of Quakers, depending largely on where they happened to live. Others were only touched indirectly through their business interests. The Society remained faithful to its testimony but did little to relate it to social problems.

The nineteenth century saw a new stirring of concern as warfare became ever more widespread and destructive in its effects. The Society was fully aroused in the period of total war,

4

which was seen as the greatest evil in the world. All manner of initiatives to prevent it and lay the foundations of peace flowered at the time. Revolutionary and far-reaching changes have affected military affairs since the middle of this century. They call for a new response from Friends and a fresh look at their activities. That will be the subject of the next chapter, but before turning to that, it might be useful to take note of some basic features of the Peace Testimony as it has developed through the centuries.

The first is one of historical determinism. For two hundred years after the end of the seventeenth century, Friends, with some notable exceptions, reacted to circumstances. They rarely took a long-term view or tried to anticipate events, except when war was imminent. To use military terminology; the first generation of Friends was on the offensive, the later generations were on the defensive. A change came at the end of the nineteenth century, when the Society set up permanent committees to keep its peace-work under constant review. During the interval between the two world wars, Friends made attempts to attack the roots of war and worked for the establishment of procedures and institutions which would lead to its avoidance and the peaceful settlement of disputes. Their thinking was strongly coloured by the optimism of an earlier age. War was attributed to particular and well defined causes, such as the arms race or economic injustice and exploitation. It was thought that if one could remove the causes, the prospect of permanent peace would be at hand.

The demonic character of Hitler and his regime came as a rude shock to many Friends, some of whom abandoned their pacifism under the impact. Since 1945, Friends have been very much on the offensive again. Their efforts have been more widespread and marked by a mixture of new diagnoses and old prescriptions.

42

A very important and easily overlooked aspect of Friends' peace activities in the nineteenth and twentieth centuries is the influence of the cultural background and the power of Britain and the United States. None of us can escape entirely from his cultural heritage. People in Europe and Asia often regard Quakerism as a peculiar Anglo-Saxon religion which cannot flourish in any other cultural milieu. This could not have been said in the early years of the movement when Quaker groups sprang up in Germany and elsewhere on the Continent. Today, outside their traditional homes in Britain and the United States, Quakers are most strongly entrenched in those areas which have been subject to British rule or have been fields of British and American missionary enterprise.

Ideas of the freedom of individual conscience, tolerance, compromise, pragmatism and the flexible application of the rule of law, seem typically English because they have been evolved painfully in this country and have become part of our philosophy of life. Secure behind their ocean ramparts and the shield provided by their navies, the British and Americans could afford to develop societies in which these characteristics became dominant. They have worked their way into Quaker thought and practice.

Our Quaker business meetings are a refinement of all these qualities. A business meeting in France or Japan could not function in quite the same way, if only because of the French tradition of rigorous and uncompromising intellectual confrontation and of the Japanese method of reaching decisions. In my work as organizer of international student seminars in Japan for the American Friends Service Committee, I started by applying my British experience in personal and group relations and unwittingly caused great offence by riding roughshod over Japanese sensibilities. It was only when I learnt and accepted that there was a Japanese way of doing things that

43

I could enter into a meaningful and deep relationship with my Japanese friends.

The other factor which influenced the outlook of Friends was the dominant part in world affairs played first by Great Britain and then by the United States. This encouraged their citizens to feel a sense of responsibility for the world. Friends, more than most, were predisposed towards this feeling and thus unconsciously shared in the Anglo-American imperialisms, especially in their missionary work. Nor could they escape from a kind of cultural imperialism in their peace work.

Images of the international system are strongly influenced by the experience and evolution of particular social systems. For example, the concept of international politics as hinging on the balance of power arose out of Europe's historical experience and was different from that of East Asia which revolved around China and reflected the structure and philosophy of Chinese society. In their action for peace, Friends have been guided by the prevalent structures and ideas of the society in which they live. Blueprints for international institutions, like the League of Nations or the United Nations, not only reflect European concepts of the international system but traditions of parliamentary democracy. Appeals for the rights of conscientious objection are often based on the assumption that a society can tolerate such deviation in time of war; an assumption which is easier to make for Englishmen or Americans, who have not been overrun by enemies, than for Frenchmen or Russians.

Another feature of Friends and their Peace Testimony is the persistence of individual witness and involvement in the world. Quakers may have been limited by their historical experience and cultural background, but that did not prevent individuals in each generation from standing out as pioneers in the attack on the scourge of war.

William Penn was the first in the line with his reasoned essay on the organization of Europe. It was not an entirely new idea, for it developed those of Henry IV and Sully, and other predecessors, making them relevant to his age. More exciting was the attempt to apply Quaker principles to the government of Pennsylvania. Alas, it was all too brief, but while it lasted it showed that fair dealing, sincerity, trust and a response to that of God in other men could be made to work in politics. There was no conflict between Pennsylvanians and Indians between 1681 and 1755. On the other hand, Penn and the Quaker-dominated assembly failed to take a consistent stand over military matters from the very beginning.[36]

John Woolman demonstrated that genuine humility and a loving approach could have revolutionary effects. He drew the moral of:

> . . . the advantage of living in the real substance of religion where practice doth harmonize with principle.[37]

He was also well aware that toleration and the absence of immediate pressures can corrupt the spirit. Compromise might lead to distinguishing Quakers as 'little else but the name of a peaceable people'.

The career of John Bright showed that a successful politician could hold the highest moral principles. It also revealed the difficulty inherent in combining absolute pacifism with political office in a non-pacifist society, as he told his constituents in Birmingham in 1858:

> I believe there is no permanent greatness to a nation except it be based on morality . . . I have not, as you have observed, pleaded that this country should remain without adequate and scientific means of defence. I acknowledge it to be the duty of your statesmen, acting upon the known opinions and principles of ninety-nine

out of every one hundred persons in the country, at all times, with all possible moderation, but with all possible efficiency, to take steps which shall preserve order within and on the confines of your kingdom.[38]

This has been the dilemma of other Quaker politicians, right up to the present. One, at least, drew the logical conclusion of his faith, though admittedly in a not very serious situation.

Eli Jones had been elected to the Maine Assembly in 1854. He fulfilled his duties conscientiously without ever speaking in the House. Partly to force him to break his silence, his colleagues, with tongues in cheek, elected him in 1855 to the office of Major-General of the not very formidable State militia. Jones explained his refusal in the following splendid statement:

It is generally understood that I entertain peculiar views in respect of the policy of war. If, however, I am an exponent of the views of the legislature on that subject, I will cheerfully undertake to serve the state in the capacity indicated. I shall stand before the militia and give such orders as I think best. The first would be: 'Ground arms.' The second would be: 'Right about face; beat your swords into ploughshares, and your spears into pruning hooks, and learn war no more.' I should then dismiss every man to his farm and to his merchandise, with an admonition to read daily at his fireside the New Testament, and ponder upon its tidings of Peace on Earth, Good Will towards men.

He thought that his election was premature and concluded:

With pleasure I now surrender to the House this trust and honour, and return to private life.[39]

Other Friends were pioneers at different levels. To cite two examples: Pierre Ceresole was the founder of the international work camp movement after the First World War, while a few decades later a group of people around the American Friends Service Committee brought officials from communist countries into a reasoned and private dialogue with their Western colleagues, long before this became a 'respectable' thing to do.

Not all of the initiatives in peace-making had the official support of the Society of Friends, which avoided a noticeably political stand on contemporary problems. It confined itself, instead, to very general statements recalling its fundamental religious position. Official Quaker pronouncements were, of course, coloured by the temper of the times as they attempted to address the great issues of the day, but their appeal always rested on a spiritual concept of the world. An outstanding example was the message from the first World Conference of Friends held in London in 1920:

> The roots of war can be taken away from all our lives, as they were long ago in Francis of Assisi and John Woolman. Day by day let us seek out and remove every seed of hatred and of greed, of resentment and of grudging in our own selves and in the social structure about us. Christ's way of freedom replaces slavish obedience by fellowship. Instead of an external compulsion He gives an inward authority. Instead of self-seeking we must put sacrifice; instead of domination, cooperation. Fear and suspicion must give place to trust and the spirit of understanding. Thus shall we more and more become friends to all men and our lives will be filled with the joy which true friendship never fails to bring. Surely this is the way in which Christ calls us to overcome the barriers of race and class and thus to make of all humanity a society of friends.[40]

These words have a truer ring than many previous statements which were often issued for the record. The Friends who issued them had suffered the experience of the World War. They spoke in the best prophetic tradition of the Society: There was the recognition of the existence of evil, of conflict, and of the need for sacrifice as part of the struggle for good. Throughout there was the conviction that the good would overcome.

Of course, one reason why the Society issued statements couched in prophetic terms was because it is easier to agree on a description of the ideal society than on the means to realise it. The exploration of ways to fulfil the promise was left to individuals or concerned groups. Before completely dimissing the formal pronouncements as vague and empty, it is as well to remember that they helped to keep a small flame alight at times when the Society was inward-turned and very much preoccupied with its own affairs. The flame, like a pilot light, ignited the spirits of individual Friends in every generation. The result was often a burst of activity that reached far beyond the confines of the small Quaker world.

Two conclusions suggest themselves from this rapid survey of the history of Friends' testimony against war. First, there is a double aspect of the testimony. It springs from a prophetic view of the world and its main expression is in humanitarian work. Second, it is necessary to keep the source of our faith constantly in sight to avoid a stifling of the spirit and the loss of that spontaneity which marked the beginnings of the Quaker movement. At the same time it is also necessary to keep the practical expression of that faith under constant review. Otherwise it might become misplaced. Times change and so does our understanding. That is why I will try to examine contemporary problems in the next chapter.

THE CONTEMPORARY WORLD

The last world war ended twenty-nine years ago and people are talking less now about the danger of a third world war than they were ten or twenty years ago. There is plenty of material lying about in terms of conflict situations and weaponry which would make the previous world war look a very limited affair indeed. This is not, therefore, a time for complacency, but it is a time for some slight hope. That hope does not rest on signs of a dramatic change in social values or of mass conversion to the gospel of love, but upon changing circumstances which are forcing men into a fundamental reappraisal of the uses of armed force.

The changes may be divided into two categories: Those that have a bearing on the international system and those that affect the patterns of conflict. In each case they do not proceed at a uniform pace, nor are they evenly spread over the world. Their effect is not pre-determined, so that they have a more or less equal potential for good or bad results. My intention is to focus on the second category of changes and their relevance to Friends' Peace Testimony, but it is important to see them against a wider background which is largely the cause of new developments and new perceptions in warfare.

The causes of war

In the preceding chapters I have referred to the inner conflict to which we are all exposed. It is a problem of personal morality and concerns our freedom to choose. The choice is not always a simple one between right and wrong, good and evil. Very often

49

it is between two rights or between two wrongs. Social and international conflicts can rarely be dealt with in terms of right and wrong. They involve clashes of interest in which the claims of each party may be perfectly legitimate when examined in terms of its own needs and security, but which are irreconcilable with similar claims made by other parties.

That does not preclude the legitimacy and even obligation of making moral choices in such disputes, but they can only be valid if made in full knowledge of the problems involved for the decision-makers. That knowledge must include recognition of the fact that states are not individuals, although the illusion that they are is strengthened by the deplorable habit of referring to them in personal terms. The process of formulating state policy is a long and complicated one, involving the accommodation of a great variety of competing and contradictory interests.

There are always several causes which may explain any international conflict, although one may stand out as the most important or most immediate. Theories about the origins of war have varied from single-cause explanations such as economic competition, or the irreconcilable interests of competing nation states, or simply the will to power, to all-inclusive and comprehensive analyses which reject such simple generalizations.[41]

The last approach is the sounder one, but having said this I propose to run the risk of over-simplification by suggesting that violent conflicts in the world today increasingly have their origins in one of three types of cause: The ever fiercer scramble for scarce resources; the aspirations of a new nationalistic self-consciousness; the social tensions of industrialized mass societies. They are obviously closely related and none can be isolated as *the* cause of a war. To cite two examples: The scramble to secure some scarce raw material may encourage certain forms of economic imperialism which run counter to the aspirations of nationalistic movements. Again, the phenomenon of nationalism in the developing areas of the world is linked to the social tensions in the industrialized mass societies. The one is a rebellion against a world system dominated by vast industrial, commercial and military interests; the other arises from a rebellion by the underprivileged and many of the young against the same domination within a society.

I do not wish to minimize the importance of the deep-rooted historical causes of some contemporary conflicts. One need only cite those in the Middle East and Northern Ireland as examples. However, the new elements I have mentioned enter into those conflicts as well and transform them, so that their eventual solution will not be merely a settlement of an historic dispute but one which must take account of a changing social and international environment.

The scramble for resources

One of the fundamental problems of the world is the prospect that the growth of its population combined with an increase in the rate of consumption brings the exhaustion of some natural resources within measurable distance and raises the question whether others, particularly food, can continue to match the demand. Can we rely on man's inventive genius and techno-logical ingenuity to develop alternative sources of food, energy and raw materials which will enable us to continue on the path of material enrichment that has been a prime motive of all human endeavour? That is the subject of debate among the specialists in the various fields concerned and their conclusions must inevitably be very tentative in the light of their incomplete knowledge and understanding of these matters. Nevertheless, the alarm has been sounded by the most eminent scientists and technologists, and the matter has become a subject of public

51

concern. The discussion over the environment and the quality of life is precisely about the problem of managing resources and social relationships in a crowded world.

Public interest, however, can have either good or bad effects. Much of the anxiety over the environment is merely an expression of ordinary selfishness that may be translated into the following terms: I want to keep my view, go and build your blocks of flats elsewhere; we don't want to be disturbed by noise and pollution, disturb another community with the airports or motorways which we want to use; keep out the immigrants because they increase pressure on housing, education and the social services, but I would not take jobs on the railways or in hospitals.

The same kind of morality applies at the international level. The pressure on oil resources and the accompanying rise in costs have led to various proposals for a common policy among the consumer countries. The Japanese are dubious about such arrangements because they think they may be able to do better on their own. They do not want to be saddled with the bad image among the oil producers that applies to the Americans and some Europeans, and they do not want to depend on the good will of international companies based on the United States and a few European powers. This lack of trust is the most important reason why any government is reluctant to depend on others in matters which are of vital interest to the welfare of the state.

When a state becomes too weak or vulnerable to go it alone, it may be driven into cooperative ventures with others. This has happened with Britain and as a result we have entered the Common Market. Although our leaders—and those of other member states—are loud in their protestations that a united Europe will become a force for peace and be open to the rest of the world, the main motive is to seek a new strength with which to resist Russian and American pressures and to compete more effectively in the world.

1984 is ten years away and there are some signs that we are moving in the direction of the Orwellian world. Among them is the creation of giant blocs which are in more or less permanent competition, each trying to be as self-sufficient as possible. However, even states which are the size of continents, like the United States and Russia, have recently experienced the limits of their self-sufficiency. Americans must import oil to keep their civilization going; Russians enter into huge commercial deals with the United States because they need American technology and grain. The Chinese, who have made self-reliance the corner-stone of their national policy, are eager to expand trade with the rest of the world and are particularly in need of foreign technology.

Another version of the ideal of self-sufficiency is the suggestion that the wealthy countries of the non-communist world should draw together to preserve their standard of life and leave the hundreds of millions in Asia, Africa and Latin America, who live far below that standard and are short of some of the basic necessities of life, to their fate. It is conceivable that North America, Europe, Japan and Australasia, could form a closed world of the 'advanced' people, but they would soon discover the shortcomings of their self-sufficiency, for they would continue to depend on other areas for oil, natural gas, various minerals and the products of tropical climates. The recent oil crisis has underlined the extreme vulnerability of the highly industrialized societies.

In short, it is most unlikely that any one country or group of countries will be successful in shutting out the problems of the world. On the contrary, their involvement with each other is likely to increase rather than diminish. Technological developments are strengthening the trend towards interdependence.

53

The so-called 'communications revolution' is one example. It enables us to know almost instantaneously of any major event in any part of the world, to promote the spread of ideas and fashions with startling rapidity, and to move over thousands of miles in a matter of hours. Here again, the effect may be harmful or beneficial.

Television is a particularly dangerous medium. It can feed simple addictive pulp into a consumer who cannot ask questions or answer back. The habit of persistent watching is even more pernicious than the content of the programmes, for it encourages a passivity which may undermine people's ability to face the realities of life.[42] Yet, television can also stimulate ideas through discussion programmes that present a very complex world and encourage a more critical view of it.

Growing interdependence need not lead to greater harmony. We know from our own personal and social experience that the more we are involved with others the greater the opportunities for friction, as well as cooperation. Thus, the demand for vital but scarce resources involves the risk of serious confrontations. The most ominous signs of a move in that direction are again noticeable in the search for sources of energy. The American, European and Japanese economies presently depend on the availability of increasing quantities of oil and natural gas. The prospect of being shut off completely from any major source of supply might provoke the most dangerous reactions.

Yet, the rivalries of today are different from the rivalries of nation states at the beginning of this century. For one thing, they may take place within and between large associations of states, which are much more than the traditional kaleidoscopic alliances. For another, the interest of the nation state as the sole determinant of the conduct of international relations may be on the decline.

At first sight, the energy crisis appears to have reversed this process in the European Community, reducing it once more to a group of squabbling and competing nation states. It would be unwise to conclude that therefore nothing has really changed. Since its foundation, the Community has passed through one crisis after another, each time in danger of coming apart at the seams. It may, of course, eventually do so, but there are powerful interests and forces at work which could equally well ensure its survival and the gradual decline of the nation state in Western Europe.

Factors like the interests of multinational economic corporations and of international and supranational institutions, or the effects of technology and environmental problems, are confusing the question of what is the national interest. Governments are increasingly forced to take them into account when formulating policy.

Nationalism

The role of ideology as a source of conflict is difficult to determine. We all know that it is often a flag under which people and interest groups fight over specific and material issues. Once those issues lose their importance or are removed, ideology may also lose its force. However, ideologies can acquire a reality of their own in the course of the struggle. They expand the conflict beyond the specific issues over which it started and carry it on long after the original problems have ceased to matter. Above all, they create an image of the world which may bear little relationship to the actual state of affairs. Because the image is mistaken for reality, it may become a major source of war.

The ideology of nationalism is still a potent source of conflict, although it is no longer marked by sabre-rattling confrontations under the slogan 'My country, right or wrong!' It is a strong force in many parts of the world, with an emotional and intellectual content that is more like the nationalism which was first kindled by the French Revolution. That is not to say it will not become expansionist and imperialist like the nationalisms of nineteenth-century Europe. Indeed, it is already happening in some areas. Jewish nationalism became expansionist. Arab nationalism is turning into economic imperialism. Vietnamese nationalism is threatening its weaker neighbours with political domination. They are examples of how an ideology, which arose in association with particular aspirations, continues to be invoked for very different objectives.

Nationalistic self-consciousness is found among minority groups in old-established states. They believe that the centralized modern governmental machine discriminates against their interests and exploits them, either because they are minorities or because they are remote from the centres of power. Hence the emergence of nationalist movements in Scotland, Wales and Brittany and among the Basques, the Blacks and the Red Indians. Nationalism is also strong among the new states which have come into being since 1945 and which enjoy legal sovereignty but still struggle with a hang-over from colonial rule or against the economic domination of foreign interests. For the progressive-minded, including many pacifists, nationalism has therefore changed from a dirty to a clean word.

Apart from the upsurge of nationalist feelings in many parts of the world, other ideologies may be losing some of their importance as sources which embitter conflict. Although anti-communist crusaders still use the quaint expression 'Free World' when talking about non-communist states, regardless of whether they refer to Holland or Greece, few in the Western countries would argue that they should try to convert the rest of the world to their own brand of democracy. We are too aware of its injustices and contradictions to be satisfied that ours is the perfect form of society.

The communist ideology still appeals to many people, but decades of malpractices and schisms have made it very difficult to know what communism is. The people of the East European states are more preoccupied with the rights of national self-determination than with adherence to any monolithic ideological system. The Russian rulers still operate within an ideological framework of reference, but their policies are principally directed to securing a state that is controlled by a faceless and oppressive bureaucracy. The Chinese are presently the most consistent in the application of ideology to the management of society, but it is significant that theirs is an essentially nationalist approach. Communism in China is the instrument for the rebirth of the country after more than a century of decline and foreign domination. The revolutionary message of the Chinese stresses that each people must find its own road to salvation. The revolution must come from within society and cannot be imported from outside.

Traditionally established religions, too, have lost their power to incite men to go to war for the faith, though sectarian bigotry still flourishes in some places. The friction between Hindu and Moslem has not prevented a predominantly Hindu India from supporting a predominantly Moslem Bangladesh in its nationalistic struggle against the remote control of a government more than one thousand miles away. Similarly, a Catholic government in Dublin and a Protestant government in London can cooperate in attempts to restrain the religious fanatics on both sides in Northern Ireland.

In the conflict between Arab and Jew, the control of Jerusalem and its Holy Places is one of the major issues between the two sides. It symbolizes the fusion of religion and nationalism in Judaism and Islam. Jewish and Moslem communities have lived peacefully side by side for centuries. They share much common ground in their beliefs, unlike Moslems and Hindus. Yet, the Arab-Israeli conflict is so embittered because the land has a religious and historic significance for both parties. There are, however, some signs that both sides in the Middle East conflict may have started on the difficult path leading to the peaceful co-existence of the Arab and Jewish nations.

The problems of mass society

Violence in our urbanized civilization must be seen against the wider problems posed by the difficulties of managing a mass society without resorting to authoritarian methods. Apart from the violence of desperate groups, there is the inclination to by-pass established procedures and take direct action over all manner of pressing social issues. Such actions range from squatting by the homeless in unoccupied houses to the occupation of factories by workers.

The revolt of May–June 1968 in France is very revealing in this respect. For a few weeks the state all but disappeared. Everyone was thrown back on his own resources and returned to the locally based social group in which there was genuine human contact. In the end the great impersonal forces of society, from giant corporations to trade unions, reassembled the machinery of control. One is tempted to see it as the dying kick of Orwell's proles against the tyranny of the technological state. That would be a gross over-simplification. It revealed the dilemmas raised by the existence of modern mass society without pointing to their solution. How can we reconcile the need for a greater sense of community within society and the need for highly complex and extensive organization to manage our technological civilization?

The significance of this and similar events, albeit on a smaller scale, is the rejection by a substantial segment of the population, especially the young, of the modern state as the main focus for their allegiance. Instead, they are looking for opportunities to identify with smaller and more human communities. The traditional institutions of society no longer satisfy this need and some of them, notably the churches, are being radically transformed under the impact of popular alienation.

There is another side to the search for new meaning in life that has led to all manner of individual and group experimentation. Some of it is futile utopianism, some is harmful to those engaged in it. The use of drugs or the craze for certain types of oriental mysticism are often little more than new forms of selfishness through which people seek to escape from the burdens of social responsibility.

These tendencies are reinforced by another factor which is weakening the hold of the state over its citizens. In the past it was able to retain their loyalty by appealing for unity in the face of apparent external threats. Today, this perception of threat is being displaced. What worries people is the threat from pollution, the threat from overcrowding, the threat of inflation. Europeans, in particular, do not feel that they are threatened by external enemies and they see little use in expensive military establishments that are wasteful of resources which could be used for improving the standard of living.

Restraints on the use of armed force

Our generation is very much aware of the infinite complexity of the phenomenon of war. Furthermore, its rising cost and the uncertainties of its outcome have injected a more coldly calculating element into inter-state relations. This attitude is epitomized by military men who frequently express doubts that their power is the answer to the problem of ensuring the supply

59

of essential raw materials. They would have had no such doubts fifty years ago.

This has not meant that governments are ready to abandon the instrument of war. All the evidence points to the opposite conclusion. It has, however, encouraged those with the most destructive weapons at their disposal to limit its use and to be more precise in defining their aims when dealing with equally powerful adversaries.

Another factor of great importance which encourages restraint is the growing understanding of the intimate relationship between the economic, social and political structure of a state and its foreign policy. This, too, has made for greater circumspection. It has led to a 'steering' concept in the conduct of foreign policy, in which manipulation of the reactions of the other party in a dispute may assume greater importance than forcing it to submit to one's will through the display of superior force.[43] The manipulative process may, of course, include the threat of resorting to the use of force.

Governments obviously intend to keep the right of going to war if what they consider to be a vital national interest is at stake. This could be the survival of the state, the preservation of some value such as the standard of living or the system of government, or the freedom to conduct an independent foreign policy. Whether they will do so is another and more open question. I have tried to suggest that the declining power of ideologies and a greater awareness of the complexities of the modern world may influence the extent to which the so-called technologically advanced states are ready to go to war.

The nationalist movements, whether in the new states or among minorities in older states, pose a very different problem. They pursue revolutionary objectives, seek popular support and are economically weak. Circumstances usually force them into low-level though often widespread forms of violence. Guerrilla warfare is not confined to the struggle of subject people in the Third World, as we know only too well with one such conflict on our own doorstep in Northern Ireland.

Such is the background against which we have to examine the nature of war today. Modern weapons and military organization both reflect and contribute to the evolution of contemporary international society.

Nuclear deterrence

The most obvious and most discussed development since 1945 has been the acquisition of nuclear and thermonuclear weapons which, for their possessors, have revolutionized concepts of defence and have modified the conduct of international relations. Such weapons have made deterrence an autonomous concept as distinct from defence.

Deterrence has always been an element of military policy. If a government had large armed forces at its disposal, it hoped that there would be no need to use them because the opponent would be sufficiently intimidated or sufficiently rational to want to avoid war at all costs. From historical experience it was axiomatic that this form of deterrence would break down from time to time, so that all attention was turned to perfecting the means of defence, which in practice often meant offence.

The qualitative change which has come about since 1945 is that, in their relations with each other, those states possessing nuclear armouries have placed most emphasis on deterrence. This means full-scale preparation for nuclear war at enormous cost, for it is essential to demonstrate that one really means business. Nevertheless, it is hoped that the show of determination will in fact make war most unlikely. Deterrence is a double-edged concept. It has the defensive connotation of preventing an opponent from aggressive action, but it can also mean that one is trying to prevent him from interfering with one's own designs.

The basic principle of deterrence strategy is to have an ability to devastate the enemy, even after he has launched an attack. The arms race between the United States and the Soviet Union turns around the second-strike capability of each side. For only if the other party is convinced that it cannot avoid destruction after launching a surprise or first-strike attack will it be deterred. The complexities of the discussion about nuclear strategy, reminiscent of the disputations of medieval school-men, need not concern us here.

Various attempts have been made by analysts and strategists to envisage nuclear warfare which could be controlled and whose damage would be limited.[44] The object of the exercise is to make deterrence more credible by integrating it with conventional military strategy and thereby to reduce the element of bluff in the whole business. Such analyses have had a significant influence on strategic thinking but they have fortunately not been put to the test so far.

The effects of war with nuclear weapons are incalculable, not least because their psychological impact is unknown, if we leave aside the experience of the relatively small bombs dropped on Hiroshima and Nagasaki. Colossal sums and immense resources are devoted to their development and perfection in the hope that they will never be used in action.

Nuclear deterrence remains essentially a psychological phenomenon, depending on the will of those who rely on it and the reaction of their opponents. It is not confined to situations of parity between the two super-powers, but also involves relationships between them and smaller nuclear powers like Britain and France. In the latter case, the question arises whether the head of the inferior state is ready to risk total destruction for the sake of meeting the attack of a superior enemy, or, alternatively, whether the stronger opponent is prepared to lose even one or two cities for the sake of imposing his will on the weaker state. Matters become more complicated if one takes into consideration the possible involvement of a third nuclear power in such a situation.

The condition of nuclear deterrence has had a two-fold effect on the policies of the nuclear powers. First, it has prevented direct armed clashes between them, if we exclude the border skirmishes between Russia and China, which have been more symbolic than serious tests of strength. The two major confrontations between the Soviet Union and the United States, over Cuba and at various times over Berlin, have been examples of a new style of diplomacy which is called crisis management. Increasingly, the deployment of military manpower by both states and their allies in Europe is seen in terms of its value in reinforcing crisis diplomacy.[45]

The second effect has been to reintroduce the concept of limited objectives in military thinking. The ideas of total victory or unconditional surrender have been abandoned and their place has been taken by the idea of limited aims. The purpose of a limited war is to achieve one's objectives without provoking a confrontation between nuclear powers.

The wars in Korea and Vietnam are good examples of this type of warfare. In both, one nuclear power, the United States, was engaged against a non-nuclear power which happened to be allied to its principal rival, the Soviet Union. The wars were carefully circumscribed by the Americans in order to avoid the risk of forcing the Russians to choose between direct intervention or appearing to desert their allies. Hence the United States did not bomb China in 1950 and restricted its bombing of North Vietnam for some years. In the latter conflict, American strategy was partly determined by the hope that awareness of this risk would compel the Russians to put

63

pressure on their allies to be more amenable to American terms.

Such wars may be limited from the point of view of the great powers, but they are certainly not so for the countries in which they are fought. They do not imply a restraint in the use of force below the nuclear threshold within the theatre of operations, as was apparent in Vietnam.

Thinking about nuclear strategy and its implications has had a significant influence on the contemporary approach to international relations. The new dimensions of warfare introduced by atomic weapons attracted the attention of those who in the past have not been directly concerned with thinking about international relations and strategy, on the grounds that these matters have now become too serious to be left to the statesmen and generals. Natural scientists, mathematicians, psychologists and economists involved themselves in discussions about the current state of the world and suggested ways of dealing with the issues raised by nuclear weapons.

The concern of natural scientists is understandable. They made such weapons possible and the more sensitive among them developed an acute sense of responsibility for the consequences. They also enjoyed great prestige as a result of the scientific and technical achievements associated with harnessing the atom to humanly controlled use. Hence, policy-makers treated them with great respect and sought their advice over matters traditionally reserved for generals, diplomats and politicians.

The scientists applied their mode of thinking to the problems of national security and came to contradictory conclusions, not because their reasoning was wrong but because they introduced value judgements into their assessments which had nothing to do with science. The advice of the hard-headed 'realist', who looked at the technical possibilities in the context of traditional power politics, advocated increased expenditure on weapons development to keep his country ahead of its enemies. The conscience-stricken 'idealist', who looked at the technical possibilities in the context of his concern for building the institutions of a lasting world peace, advocated various measures of disarmament. The dangers did not lie in their differing conclusions, but in that they were thought to be endowed with special authority because scientists had reached them. In fact, they were a group of people participating in the political process in which their discipline was an inadequate guide.[46]

The same criticism may be applied to the contribution of thinkers from other fields of expertise. The work of Thomas Schelling is an outstanding example. A mathematical economist by training, he wrote a series of interesting studies on the strategy of nuclear deterrence, which made an intellectual contribution to our understanding of the theoretical concepts involved but which had an unfortunate effect on strategists and policy-makers.[47] The application of the rather neat bargaining theories which he and others evolved accounted to some extent for the American disaster in Vietnam. The enemy simply did not play the game according to the rules and I have always thought that if the Americans had sent a team of experts to Hanoi, equipped with the appropriate computers and fully versed in the theories of Schelling and in Kahn's strategy of escalation, they might have done better in the war. At least, the North Vietnamese would then have known how they should have responded to the American moves.

One of the most telling criticisms of the work of Kahn and Schelling and their disciples was made by Philip Green in his book, *Deadly Logic*.[48] He points to some obvious weaknesses in their approach; such as Kahn's basic assumptions about rationality in decision-making; the use of false analogies by both Kahn and Schelling, particularly the latter's use of examples from child-rearing to illustrate his strategic theories; the inadequate data and unverifiable assumptions on which Kahn bases his arguments; the fact that the literature on deterrence almost completely ignores domestic political conditions as factors in the deterrence system. From our point of view, the most important attack is on the claim that the technical expertise of the theorists is morally neutral.

Green exposes the euphemisms in which deterrence theory is clothed, with their effect of obscuring ethical problems. Moreover, there are some distinct ethical assumptions behind deterrence theory which presume that no conduct is absolutely prohibited, that all violence and destruction is qualitatively indistinguishable, that a commitment to the possibility of wreaking destruction on foreign populations is morally neutral. In addition, the effect of deterrence theory is to subordinate all political considerations to military ones. Finally, he suggests that it is culture-bound in that it shares the most important American Cold War biases. One may agree with him that this is so, but not with the example of the Cold War, which is not a particular phenomenon of American culture. Deterrence theory is culture-bound because it arises from the American tendency to reduce all issues to problems of technology.

In brief, theorising about nuclear deterrence has had the welcome effect of reinforcing the circumspection and caution of policy-makers because they have become aware of the dangerous games they play. On the other hand, it has had the undesirable effect of introducing unwarrantable assumptions of rationality and objectivity into the conduct of security policies, thereby helping to obscure moral problems.

Contemporary warfare and military organization

Nuclear weapons have also influenced indirectly the patterns of contemporary warfare and military organization. Open warfare between the technologically advanced states of the world has almost disappeared, whereas it has flourished among the so-called underdeveloped countries.

A study was published in June 1968, in which the author analysed the numbers and types of armed conflict in the twentieth century. In this context he defined conflict as:

> . . . a situation where the regular armed forces of a country or community are involved (either on both sides, or on one side only) and where weapons of war are used by them with intent to kill or wound over a period of at least one hour.[49]

Taking the time-span of 1896–1967 and using the year 1939 as a dividing point between the two halves of the period, he reaches some interesting conclusions. Altogether, 128 conflicts are identified, 84 of which came after 1939. Only 28 of this number took the form of inter-state fighting, while the remaining 56 could be defined as 'armed insurgency', 'civil war' or military 'coups d'état', all of which aimed at changing governments. The corresponding figures for the period before 1939 were 24 and 20.

A further analysis in terms of geographical area of the conflicts taking place after 1945, reveals that 75 took place in the underdeveloped regions of the world: Asia, the Middle East, Africa and Latin America, while only six were located in Europe, in which I include Cyprus. Many developed states were, of course, directly involved in the armed struggles of the underdeveloped regions.

Events since 1968 do not seem to have contradicted this pattern. It seems, therefore, that the typology and geographical spread of armed conflict supports several trends I commented on earlier. Advanced technological and scientific states are inhibited from waging war against each other, but not from interfering in weaker and underdeveloped states where social and nationalist ferment are fruitful sources of armed conflict.

Technological changes—particularly the advent of nuclear weapons—have shifted the emphasis from the mobilization base to instant readiness. Among powers possessing nuclear weapons, it is no longer so important whether a country has the economic and industrial potential which can be turned into a gigantic war machine for a long protracted conflict. It is, however, essential that it can strike instantly and with full force. There has been a corresponding shift in some Western countries from mass armies, built on conscription and years of service in the reserves, which will be mobilized on the eve of war, to smaller highly trained professional forces capable of being deployed at a few hours' notice.

Conscription lingers on in Europe, partly for ideological reasons. It is intended to assure some form of credible defence as a support to nuclear deterrence, rather than to provide large reserves of trained manpower. In Western countries its effectiveness is sapped by a general disbelief in the danger of war and a corresponding unwillingness to bear the economic and financial burdens it imposes. This is not true of the totalitarian regimes of East Europe, where public pressure is much weaker though not wholly absent.

The structure of the armed forces is the central issue of the defence debate in the West. There are three models to choose from: The all-volunteer force; the conscript-citizen army; a mix of hard-core professional units backed by militia-type forces. Each has its advocates and each has its weaknesses. Volunteer forces are difficult to raise in consumer-oriented societies where the material well-being of the individual is the prime objective. Conscript armies are unpopular because they waste the time of young men in activities which are regarded as useless and unnecessary. Militia forces would be difficult to organize for the same reasons as above. Not only is there no strong perception of an external threat among the population at large, but, perhaps more significant in the long run, the traditional concept of the nation state no longer commands the respect of many young people.

The situation is again different in the non-nuclear environment of the Third World. Some conflicts, such as those between Israel and its Arab neighbours, or between India and Pakistan, are still conducted by conventional forces. Many more take the form of 'people's wars' and other types of insurgency, largely carried out by guerrillas operating among the civilian population and outwardly indistinguishable from it. This type of warfare is closely related to the nationalist and social movements I have discussed earlier. Precisely because they struggle for self-determination and freedom from external controls, they are without the formal apparatus of the state, including well established, equipped and conventionally organized armed forces.

The character of the guerrilla movements and the fact that they are fighting against established authority largely determines their means of violence. Those that have powerful friends abroad do not benefit from their direct intervention because of the fear of unleashing a major war. So the struggle is waged at a local and low level. Terror bombing, the taking of hostages, assassination and sabotage are the main tactics in the early stages of an insurrection. Once the guerrillas establish a base, their strategy becomes mixed and includes both clandestine and more open military operations. The object is to increase the general sense of insecurity and to encourage the authorities to become ever more oppressive, so that more and more people turn against them. The polarization of society leaves a diminishing margin for independent action or judgement. The greater the violence the more difficult the task of those who seek reconciliation within the community, as became tragically apparent in Vietnam and Northern Ireland.

Neither peace nor war

Deterrence and guerrilla war are thus the major features at each end of the spectrum of organized violence. Neither is a new concept, but modern technology has added new dimensions to both. The total effect of the trends which I have tried to summarize has been to de-institutionalize war. There is no longer a clear demarcation between war and peace. There have been many armed conflicts since 1945, but usually no formal declaration of war. Many wars have come to an end since 1945, but few have been followed by a formal peace treaty.

The Second World War ended with peace treaties between the victors and only the lesser members of the Axis: Italy, Hungary, Rumania, Bulgaria and Finland. The Treaty of San Francisco between Japan and its former enemies is significant because some of the most important belligerents were among those that did not sign it. Although a joint declaration at the end of 1956 established peace between the USSR and Japan, the two countries are still without a formal peace treaty. Technically, there is no peace between Germany and the victors of the Second World War; there is no peace in Korea, none between India and Pakistan, none between Israel and the Arab states. There are only cease-fires and armistices.

The settlement which brought the war in Vietnam to a halt on January 27, 1973, is noteworthy on two counts. It was an 'Agreement on ending the war and restoring peace in Vietnam', thus combining the functions of a cease-fire and a step by step approach to establishing peace. It was a programme of action rather than a definitive settlement. Events since then have underlined the difficulties not only of defining the conditions of peace but also of agreeing on the *modus operandi* which would pacify the country.

No state is willing to be seen as formally starting a war, however good its cause, nor is it willing to commit itself to formal peace. The expression 'Cold War' is a significant one. It rejects open armed conflict and formal peace. It implies a condition of hostility marked by threats, propaganda, sabotage and subversion. Increasingly, too, international and civil wars become confused. The conflicts in Korea, Vietnam, Cyprus, between India and Pakistan in 1971, are symptomatic of this trend.

Finally, the combined effect of the general international situation, the changes in the nature of armed confrontation and the rationalization about it has made our age acutely aware of the existence of conflict at all social levels. The impatient or despairing often regard violence as essential to promote desired changes.

The management of international conflict is the concern of two schools of thought which approach the problem from diametrically opposed points of view. One school holds that the resolution of any conflict ultimately rests on force and is therefore a trial of strength between the contestants. Such strength is not confined to military power but can rest as much on economic, ideological or political power. Its success depends on the skill and degree with which appropriate force can be brought to bear at the right time. That is the function of strategy, whose classical definition was limited to the use of military force:

> The art of distributing and applying military means to fulfil the ends of policy.[50]

The other school of thought is concerned with exploring ways of resolving such conflicts peacefully. The object is to reach an accommodation between conflicting interests which cannot be fully reconciled. Their partial satisfaction is considered preferable to the satisfaction of neither party or the recourse to a trial of strength. This approach relies on the recognition of the existence of an overriding common interest to avoid the use of force.

The technology of modern warfare has made sole reliance on military power an increasingly hazardous means of defending or asserting the national interest. Hence, it is used as a background to the exercise of other forms of power. This has become the subject of serious study of all those concerned with national security, but their image of the international system is still one of the anarchic confrontation of states which must in the end rely on the manipulation of their strength for survival.

Strategic thought, which was once the exclusive preserve of the military, is now applied to almost any realm and we talk of economic, political or social strategies. Under its impact, the idea of promoting harmony through the reconciliation of conflicting interests and cooperative effort is relegated to secondary importance. This type of thinking may be found in the works of General André Beaufre,[51] in which he analyses international relations with the tools of the strategic method. It strengthens the assumption that relations between states are essentially hostile and based on threats, thus ruling out the legitimate diplomatic concern for compromise and accommodation.

The military profession

The developments described above have naturally been accompanied by changes in concepts of the military profession and in the organization of military establishments. The traditional pacifist idea of the military is lagging behind reality. Much of the peace literature conveys an image of brutal, depraved and unprincipled men who have no souls and are bent on the oppression and destruction of the innocent. Granted that the armed services attract a number of men who glory in violence and who are unprincipled adventurers, one can also point to a very different type of soldier who has a tender conscience.

I have noted that a surprising number of the early Friends had military backgrounds. There have been many examples since of soldiers who have turned their attention to the work of healing and reconciliation. Some, even, have become convinced of non-violence. An outstanding recent example is General Paris de Bollardière, who had a distinguished record with the Free French during the war and was a parachute officer in the Foreign Legion—an élite unit which acquired considerable notoriety in the Algerian war. In August 1957, he was sentenced to sixty days' imprisonment for having publicly supported M. Jean-Jacques Servan-Schreiber's denunciation of torture in Algeria. At his own request he was prematurely retired from active service in 1961 and placed in the reserve. He has become a convinced opponent of French nuclear armament on pacifist grounds and was on board the vessel 'Fri' which sailed as a protest into the French nuclear test zone in 1973. For this he was compulsorily retired from the army.

Such action has to be set against the actions of others like those responsible for the massacre at My Lai. It merely illustrates the point that the spirit may move among military men as freely as among others. It is perhaps all the more remarkable that it does so in a profession whose function is not only to manage violence but which has in the past placed emphasis on unquestioning obedience to the commands of others as the first duty of its members.

In discussing the various elements which make up the traditional military ideal, Professor Huntington wrote that:

The military ethic is thus pessimistic, collectivist, historically inclined, power-oriented, nationalistic, militaristic, pacifist, and instrumentalist in its view of the military profession. It is, in brief, realistic and con-servative.[52]

From that list it seems that all one can do is pay one's money and take one's choice. Quite obviously, the relative strength with which the different facets of the ethic are held will vary from individual to individual.

The main characteristics of the professional ethos in modern times have been devotion to one's country, a belief that military force is essential to its security, but that its exercise should be avoided as much as possible. If it does become necessary it should be managed economically and should be commensurate with the objective. The conversion of the holder of such a set of ideas to non-violence must be the result of a profound inner revolution. Nevertheless, even those who do not experience it can be alive to the need of bringing military power under control and making its use less likely. A glance at some of the soldiers who have been involved at various times in efforts to strengthen the institutions of peace through the United Nations can tell us that.

Events since 1945 have brought about changes in the composition, function and outlook of the military profession of the technologically advanced countries that mark a break with the past and open up new vistas of the soldier's role.

In countries like Britain and the United States, the motives for entering upon a military career are changing. Appeals to patriotism, to doing one's duty to the country, to honour, to heroism and self-sacrifice are no longer made. Instead, the recruiting propaganda lays stress on the opportunities of a good career, of acquiring skills that will be useful in civilian life at a later stage, on the ability to exercise one's initiative, to which is added the bonus of perhaps a little travel and some adventure.

The skills required today are of a highly technical order and both weapons and military organization call for managerial competence rather than heroic virtues. The technical officer is beginning to erode the traditional primacy of the officer in the so-called teeth arms. For one thing, he has skills which often enable him to transfer to another profession in mid-career with comparative ease. The syllabuses of cadet schools and staff colleges are moving away from the study of military history and military drill. Instead, they attempt to provide a broad general education with a bias towards scientific subjects and an understanding of the social and international environment. There is a marked trend towards offering a university-type education to the officer.

These are only some examples of a development which is narrowing the gap between the soldier and the civilian. In some countries, notably the Federal Republic of Germany, the notion of the citizen in uniform includes the right of soldiers to belong to trade unions and to become candidates in municipal elections. The training of the contemporary German soldier is based on 'Innere Führung'. This fascinating and untranslatable concept includes several ideas. Among them is the denial of the traditional view of a sharp distinction between the civil and military functions. Discipline should be limited to the minimum necessary for making the military apparatus work. There is to be no superfluous drill and form. Most important is the belief that the soldier is not a cog in a machine, that he has basic human rights, that he has freedom of discussion, that he has to make decisions for himself and to use his moral judgement. In sum, the soldier has the right to the full development of his personality so long as it is compatible with the efficient execution of his duties.[53] In place of the preoccupation with the danger that the whole of society will be turned into a military camp, which was very understandable in the age of total war, we now have the phenomenon in reverse: The civilizing of the military.

The same trend may be observed in decision-making at the governmental level. The military are still asked for their advice on matters of national security and they still cannot get enough hardware for their purposes. But their voices are no longer so loud in the babble raised by scientists, technologists, economists, industrialists, civil servants and academic strategists, who all have something to say about the needs and problems of national security.

In the Western democracies there has been steady progress since 1945 in reducing the importance of the uniformed personnel and the separate armed services through the centralization of defence organization and planning and the establishment of vast civilian bureaucracies to control them. In part this was a reaction against the enormous influence exercised by the chiefs of staff, particularly in the United States, during the Second World War, and to the wastefulness of allocating scarce economic resources to competing services, fighting for the lion's share, especially when it comes to managing the very expensive strategic deterrent. Yet, it also reflected the increasing difficulty of deciding where the military aspect of national security ends and where its civilian aspect begins.

The arms industry

Another example of the approximation of the military and civilian spheres is to be found in the place occupied by the modern arms industry in the national economy. This factor has always been the subject of lively concern among pacifists. Quite apart from the question whether armaments are a major cause of war, there are the issues of the diversion of resources from peaceful use and the element of profit in the arms trade, which is peculiarly repugnant. The great private merchants of death, who dominated the scene before the First World War and in the inter-war period, have been replaced by governments. They have not been backward in pushing the sale of arms. At first this was seen as a means of influencing the buyer country and tying it to one's own security system. This view was particularly strong during the Cold War period, when a switch in the source of supply was seen as a major set-back for the displaced supplier. Thus, the sale of communist-made arms to Egypt and the American response to it marked a major shift of alignments in the Middle East.

The effectiveness of exercising influence or control over a country's policy by these means has lately been questioned. Non-aligned countries have deliberately chosen to rely on several suppliers and they have not always conformed to a supplying power's wishes. Indeed, the Russians and the Americans have each experienced difficulties in controlling their clients in the Middle East, so they have reached the sensible conclusion that it is best to combine their efforts to manage the situation in that region.

The production of arms has assumed a new importance in the past few years as a key element in the national economy. It is often fostered and justified on the grounds that it stimulates advanced technology and thereby helps to place national industry in a competitive position. Some of the arguments for the development of nuclear weapons have been based on the spin-off effect for civilian industry. The contention is that no private commercial enterprise could afford to invest the large amounts of capital required in projects whose profitability must perforce remain in doubt. Therefore, it is necessary to benefit from the resources available through the defence establishment.

77

The validity of the argument is in doubt, but it sometimes enables governments to push through expensive development projects which would have been strongly resisted if the declared intention had been to devote them solely to military ends.

The trade in arms is also an important factor in promoting a favourable balance of payments. The fierce competition in the international arms market arises from the need to finance extremely expensive projects, which could not be justified by the domestic market alone, and from the overall concern with the export drive. Countries like France and Britain are especially attracted by the prospect of substantial arms sales abroad. Not only do they make no distinction between the regimes to which they sell weapons, but they may even contradict security interests. The sale of British Harrier aircraft to Spain via the United States in 1973 is a case in point. The advantages of such a deal apparently outweighed the disadvantages of arming a country which had laid claim to British territory.

The military and society

All this is further evidence of the blurring of distinctions between military and non-military affairs. National security has become an all-embracing concern in which purely military policy can no longer be isolated from the other spheres of national policy and, indeed, is declining in importance. It is often held that these developments are symptomatic of the militarization of society, or, to use a more fashionable term, indicate that it is dominated by a military-industrial complex.

According to Professor Andreski, a society becomes militarized when it is extensively controlled by the military, who subordinate its needs to those of the armed forces.[54] That would not be an accurate description of what is happening in the advanced states. If we think of the military as the uniformed services, they have lost a great deal of the power and influence they enjoyed in the age of total war. They are under the control of civilian authorities in both democratic and totalitarian states.

Yet, the international environment and modern weapons and warfare have created a situation which favours the subordination of society's needs to the interests of security in its broadest sense. The adaptation of strategic thinking to policy and the large dependence of the economy on the arms industry are two examples of this process. However, it would not necessarily be true to see in this proof of the existence of a military-industrial complex. People with a military background have become increasingly involved in the management of all sectors of the economy in some countries. It does not follow that they will manage it in the interests of the armed services or even defence. It may mean simply that they form an important, if not the major, element in a new civilian administrative-technocratic élite which is primarily interested in the exercise of power through the machinery of the state.

There is, of course, the other disturbing element of the proliferation of militarily controlled regimes all over the world, particularly in Asia, Africa and Latin America. In so far as that phenomenon concerns us here, it should be remembered that military *coups d'état* are by no means always followed by the militarization of society. Their significance is related more to the problems of cohesion and government in states where other social institutions are weak or non-existent. They are often a manifestation of class struggle against the traditional ruling élite. In many instances, as in Syria or Iraq, the ruling juntas are no more than politicians in uniform.

VISION AND PRACTICE

You may well ask what the preceding discussion has to do with an examination of the Quaker testimony against war. The prospect of fiercer competition for limited resources, the existence of weapons of mass destruction and their continual perfection, the spread of strategic thinking with its focus on threats and the use of force, the widespread readiness to resort to violence to redress social and political grievances, the all-embracing nature of national security, the key role of the arms industry in the national economy, and the readiness of the armed forces to take over the government in many countries, add up to a depressing catalogue of trends which face those who work for a better world.

Nonetheless, the situation includes an element of slight hope because the world, like England in the seventeenth century, is passing through a stage of rapid development. At such times, the inadequacy of established institutions, of traditional patterns of social conduct and modes of thought, opens the way for initiatives and the exercise of what Kenneth Barnes has called 'The Creative Imagination'.[55] Friends have new opportunities in which to assert their prophetic message and combine it with activities which are relevant to the immediate problems in hand.

New opportunities in current trends
The opportunities arise from some of the trends I have tried to analyse. The most important is also the most elusive. There are signs, particularly among the younger generation, that people

are turning away from the state as the object of their primary loyalty. Instead, they are transferring it to smaller, more human and vital communities of all kinds. If this evidence is confirmed, it is of central importance because the whole apparatus of military security is inseparable from the existence of the modern state. However, the trends are not yet clear and the significance is in question.

There are other developments about which one can speak with more certainty. First is the blurred distinction between war and peace, with the accompanying shift from concentration on only one form of conflict to the problem of conflict in general and at all social levels. Then there is the effect of nuclear deterrence which has exposed the limits of armed force and has raised questions about its utility. Finally, the narrowing differential between the soldier and the civilian, as well as the discussion over new functions for the soldier, are breaking down the sharp division between the military and non-military spheres in society.

The lack of any clear distinction between peace and war in our times has had the effect of moving attention away from the arbitrary division in international relations between what was called the state of peace, in which the relationship of states was supposed to have been governed by one set of criteria, and what was called the state of war, in which the relationship was based on a different set of criteria. The distinction was useful because it led to the formulation of laws of war designed to protect the innocent and helpless and to preserve some humanity in the conduct of the combatants.[56] Its weakening has been accompanied by an indiscriminate use of violence and a disregard for the rights of the individual.

Under the pressure of these changes, we are paying more attention to the problems of conflict and to the processes which govern social and political change. The word 'Peace' itself has become an empty political slogan under the cover of which everyone goes to war. We all fight for peace and the notion has become as absurd as that of the 'Free World'.

More fundamentally, our concept of peace is culture-bound. A brief examination of its original meaning in different cultures and religions will show the futility of using it in the belief that everyone will understand our meaning and can agree to it. Such an examination was undertaken by Professor Takeshi Ishida. In a short but penetrating article[57] he illustrates his analysis with the following table:

Culture	Emphasis			
	The Will of God, Justice	Prosperity	Order	Tranquillity of mind
Ancient Judaism	shālōm			
Greece		eirene		
Rome			Pax	
China (Japan)			ho p'ing or p'ing ho (heiwa)	
India				śānti

Ishida takes care to warn us that it is an over-simplification, ignoring similarities at the expense of differences. It is only intended to present the differences of emphasis. He also suggests that the tendency to 'fight for peace' and to take positive action to realize justice depends to some extent where the emphasis is placed. Thus he explains why different traditions have led to different approaches towards non-violent direct action. Referring to the cultural backgrounds of India and the United States, for instance, he described the tasks which faced Gandhi and Martin Luther King:

> Gandhi had to teach non-violent *direct* action and King had to teach *non-violent* direct action.

A recognition that peace is not just the opposite of war, but that it is a word loaded with deep and complex meanings helps to bridge the gap between pacifists and non-pacifists, especially at a time when war between nuclear powers has become a very dubious instrument of policy. There is considerable heart-searching among military men and those concerned with national security about the place of military force in national policy and the role of the armed services in society.

The position of Japan underlines the problem in a fascinating way. It is the first modern state to renounce war as an instrument of policy in its constitution. It is true that this was largely on the insistence of the United States and has to some extent become a dead letter, again partly on the insistence of the United States. Nevertheless, Japan is one of the world's important powers and has only developed a relatively modest armed force whose functions are strictly circumscribed. It may be argued that this is because of the security afforded by the alliance with the United States. That condition may not last for much longer and the question remains whether the Japanese will go the way of all the previous great powers and substantially increase their military strength. The answer is still wide open and there are good reasons why Japan may seek to be influential in a different manner.

This kind of questioning did not arise among the military and those responsible for national security in the past. The inevitability of war was taken for granted, although most states did their best to avoid it happening to them. Soldiers and sailors, in particular, thought war inevitable but were never quite ready for it. For one thing, they disliked war because it spoiled armies and ruined navies.

Social, political and technological factors have further contributed to a fundamental reappraisal of what we mean by national security. They have introduced military thinking and planning into many spheres of society, but they have also reduced the extraordinary status of the profession of arms. The gradual osmosis of the military and civilian spheres has both good and bad effects. It can lead to excessive concentration on the arms industry in the interests of the economy, but it can also stimulate new thinking about the function of the soldier, which sees him as doing a job, like any other person, without the traditional glamour or élitism.

One function that is much talked and written about is that of the constabulary, in which the military become an element of peaceful conflict resolution and not merely a means with which to wage conflict. I have referred to their role in reducing the risk of general war in crisis management. To this we must add the many forms of peace-keeping under the auspices of the United Nations, whether in the capacity of observers, of a barrier between two hostile camps, or of forces preserving order while attempts are made to settle a conflict by other means. In Vienna there is an International Peace Academy under the direction of an Indian officer, General Rikhye, who had been military adviser to the Secretary-General of the United Nations. The purpose of this institution is to introduce diplomats and other officials to the problems of peace-making through study and simulation exercises.

There are other examples of a widening of horizons. A book was published a few years ago,[58] which is a bridge between traditional pacifism and the 'realist' approach to international relations. It is a symposium which describes the different situations, ranging from all kinds of external military attack to the military *coup* or the establishment of totalitarian systems, in which non-violent techniques might be adopted. The organization and techniques of civilian defence are examined with reference to case studies of past attempts to use the strategy. What is particularly interesting about the enterprise is the collaboration of pacifists and distinguished military thinkers and analysts, who take each other's points of view seriously. In another area we may point to the establishment by the Ministry of Defence of a lectureship in the Ethical Problems of War, in my Department at the University of London King's College. The purpose is not to have a tame philosopher in residence who provides sophisticated arguments in support of war, but to encourage independent and rigorous enquiry into the many moral issues raised by it.

All these factors and developments give us a chance to terminate the *dialogue des sourds* which has bedevilled relations between pacifists and non-pacifists in the past. They also enable us to escape from the intellectual ghetto of pacifism.

Three main areas of service

Given the kind of people that Quakers are, there will always be individuals and groups within the Society who feel called upon to put their main efforts into the work of promoting a better world. The extent and nature of their involvement depend on the prompting of the spirit in their hearts. But they are also influenced by the make-up of their personalities, by tradition, and by their immediate environment, including current fashions of thought.

Bearing these limitations in mind, we may discern three main areas in which Friends are particularly active today. I list them without implying any order of importance. One is the development of institutions which will help to create a world system within which conflict may be settled in an orderly and preferably non-violent manner, very much as most personal and group disputes are settled within a state. The second is the application of non-violent techniques to conflict situations and to the creation of new communities. The third is the scholarly search for a better understanding of the sources of conflict and of its resolution.

The areas are not watertight compartments. They overlap and work in one will impinge on another. However, it is usual for an individual to devote most of his energies to one or other of the three approaches. What is most distressing is the temptation to assume that one's own activities are more important and superior to those of others. This arrogance is quite unwarranted if one looks at all closely at the three lines of approach.

Disarmament and international organization

Those who concentrate on building international institutions and formulating procedures for their conduct have an ancient lineage. Within the Society their ancestry goes back to the first attempts to devise instruments and methods for the peaceful settlement of international disputes. They have had their heyday in the era of total war, to which they opposed the concept of total peace through the establishment of international organizations and the promotion of world disarmament. They advocated ideas which have been widely accepted today, but that have been modified in the course of experience.

International organization is no longer seen as a straight path to world government. Indeed, it is most unlikely that world government can emerge at present or within the next few decades—if ever—except as a result of the establishment of a world empire which, more likely than not, would be some form of tyranny. However, the expansion of international institutions at all levels and the patient work to make states accept specific rules of conduct create a web of relationships and obligations that may gradually foster a tendency on the part of governments and individuals to think globally rather than nationally or regionally.

Several problems attend work in this field. First, institutional arrangements easily become dated and inadequate in a changing world situation. Some may always have been irrelevant through our faulty understanding of the system. Thus, over-emphasis on disarmament mistakes the symptom for the cause. A short while ago, a well-meaning effort tried to mobilize the Society in support of a campaign for disarmament. It was not particularly effective. Although few would dispute that general and comprehensive disarmament would be a very desirable state of affairs, few apparently believe that it can be realised for the time being. The very fact that all governments pay lip-service to it should warn us against placing too much hope that it is a practicable course in the current state of the world.

Before throwing ourselves whole-heartedly into general campaigns of this type, we have to ask whether disarmament is possible and whether it would do more than relieve superficial tensions. How can we be sure that in a disarmed world a state or group of people would not secretly rearm? How would disarmament be enforced? These questions raise problems of control which might run counter to the cherished desire for self-determination. In any event, the removal of sophisticated modern weapons might simply mean a return to more primitive ways of fighting. Reductions in armaments would have the advantage of freeing resources for constructive and humanitarian purposes, but how can we be sure that would happen? So far, the effect of reducing military expenditure has not been to increase substantially the funds available for helping the poor.

Scholars and specialists have carefully analysed the limitations of the assumptions behind and the arguments for the concept of agreed multilateral disarmament, but the disarmers have failed to come up with really convincing answers. In sum, general and comprehensive disarmament implies a revolutionary change of values in the world. Let us draw attention to its advantages by all means, but unless there is a more radical change in the outlook of men and in the structure of political institutions, it is not likely to be a very persuasive argument by itself.

In order to overcome the difficulties in achieving multilateral disarmament, it is suggested that unilateral disarmament might be a way out. It would have the advantage of starting the process without the long and tedious business of first persuading other states to sit down to disarmament negotiations and then of finding some measure of agreement from which the best one could hope for is a series of compromises and half-measures.

The advocates of unilateral disarmament have concentrated on nuclear weapons. Their objective is twofold: To demonstrate that the disarming state has turned its back on the immorality of nuclear armament and to persuade others to follow its example. This is a matter of faith and perfectly legitimate, provided it is made clear that other countries may not wish to do the same and that this could have very unpleasant consequences for the disarmed state. For example, a French or British decision to disarm unilaterally may have little effect on the super-powers and tempt the Russians to exercise greater pressure on Western Europe. A unilateral disarmament by the United States or Russia could destabilize their relationship in such a way that it might tempt the other super-power to make a bid for world domination.

Because wholesale disarmament, whether multilateral or unilateral, is seen as utopian, more and more attention is being paid to measures of arms control as offering a step by step approach to substantial disarmament. There have been some successes, particularly in the nuclear field, but here, too, there are dangers. For one thing, arms control does not necessarily mean disarmament. It may mean the stabilizing or institutionalizing of an arms race. Then, and this is the fear of the rest of the world about the strategic arms limitation talks between the United States and the Soviet Union, it could mean the attempt to freeze the international system because it favours the great powers.

That is also the problem for all who seek to strengthen the instruments of international law and international organizations. In practice it could mean no more than maintaining the *status quo* and preserving those injustices from which there seems no escape but the resort to violence. The control of the United Nations by the United States and its principal allies in the decade after the war certainly did not commend the organization to many people. To take another example from the international oil industry: International agencies, like the UN, the World Bank and the International Monetary Fund, can become tools in the hands of their major contributors and exercise an indirect influence on the economies of the poorer countries. In the past they have opposed the growth of public investment in the oil industry; they have had a penchant for a deflationary fiscal policy; and they have shied away from controversial issues such as nationalisation or petroleum pricing.[59]

Institutions, legal systems and procedures have to take the present state of affairs as their starting point. The world is far from perfect and those who work in this field try to improve it just a little. Their assumptions are well described by Montesquieu in his comments on international law:

> The law of nations is naturally founded on this principle,
> that different nations ought in time of peace to do one

another all the good they can, and in time of war as little injury as possible, without prejudicing their real interests.[60]

Work based upon that principle often requires a choice not between what is right and wrong but between what is better and what is worse. This point was driven home to me when I was engaged with a group of Friends in trying to promote a change in the representation of China at the United Nations. It seemed obviously right that the effective government of more than seven hundred million Chinese should be seated in the United Nations and thus drawn into full membership of the world community. It would mean the withdrawal of the government of Taiwan and, more important, the tacit if not open admission that Taiwan is a part of China and should in due course pass under the control of the Government in Peking. To have insisted that the fourteen million native Taiwanese, who have been cut off from the Mainland since 1895 and are now ruled by refugees from the Mainland, should be able to decide for themselves as to whether they wanted to be ruled by one group of Chinese or another, or to become an independent state, would have been wholly unacceptable to the Peking Government and, for that matter, to the one in Taipei as well. In the circumstances it seemed better to further the cause of improved international relations by having China in the United Nations than to give the Taiwanese the right of self-determination.

Non-violence

The proponent of non-violent revolutionary action seeks to avoid these compromises and prevarications by going straight to the heart of the matter. He rejects the system and tries to deal with social and political problems, using methods which stem from a different source. History is littered with the wreckage of attempts to create ideal communities governed by the spirit of love and selfless cooperation. Some have been remarkably successful in being faithful to their principles for a considerable period of time. But, sooner or later, these efforts have broken down either through pressure from within the community or from the world around it. The basic weakness of all such attempts has been to assume that the natural goodness of men would result in the creation of a good society.

Quakers would argue that the Light of Christ shines in all human beings. People are, therefore, naturally moral. However, it is not our mythical natural state but our social relations which make us aware of moral problems. Founders of ideal communities too often overlook the ambivalence of human nature and the fact that once social institutions have been created they become moralizing influences and by their very existence impose restrictions on the freedom of the individual.

Attempts to apply non-violent methods to conflict situations raise another set of problems. As I have suggested earlier, such methods are now receiving attention from people who do not share our basic Quaker assumptions. They merely see non-violence as a method which might be more economical or more effective in defeating the enemy than traditional methods of warfare. There are many historical examples of the use of non-violent methods. Most have broken down, but some have been quite successful, such as the Norwegian campaign for separation from Sweden.

For the great teachers of non-violence it has been an inseparable part of their philosophy of life and they accepted suffering, apparent failure and death rather than abandon it. To be their true disciples requires not only a revolution in social values but an inner revolution. Gandhi saw this clearly and in his later years spoke frequently of his failure. The aftermath of independence revealed how few of his followers had made non-violence an integral part of their lives, although its methods were remarkably effective when used against the British.

Past failures in the practice of non-violence are no reason to abandon it. On the contrary, it is a prophetic vocation, which cannot be judged by contemporary standards of success. The error is to try to justify it on those terms.

Study and research

The reformer and the revolutionary are joined by the thinker and the scholar in the attack on war and violence. The same reasons that brought scholars from many different disciplines into the field of strategic studies, has brought them into the wider field of international relations and conflict studies. The world appears to have reached a stage where there is a risk that it will be destroyed unless war is brought under control. This has become a problem of concern to all and not merely to the traditional experts in international relations.

A Quaker, Lewis Fry Richardson, who was a mathematician, statistician and psychologist, helped to pioneer new approaches to the study of war.[61] Friends also took the initiative recently in establishing the first Chair of Peace Studies in Britain, at the University of Bradford. Another approach has been through the social analysis of conflict, which has revealed that it can be positively functional or disruptive, depending on the types of issues over which it is fought and the social structure within which it occurs. In loosely structured societies, like the liberal or social democracies, conflicts can have stabilizing and integrative functions. They can revitalize existent norms and contribute to the emergence of new ones. In closely structured societies, such as totalitarian systems, there is a tendency to suppress conflict or to release tension by providing substitute objects upon which to vent hostile sentiments. The effect of the outbreak of conflict within such societies is often disruptive.[62]

93

The fruits of these investigations and the methods by which they are carried out can contribute to our understanding of the functioning of the international system, of the causes of war and of the ways in which it may be avoided. But the application of the mathematical, psychological and social sciences is nowhere near the formulation of a comprehensive theory of war which either tells us something new or provides a useful framework for the guidance of the practitioners of international relations. The international system is far too complex and involves elements peculiar to itself that defy easy formulations or prescriptions about how it works and how it can be managed.

In the first wave of crusading zeal, the conflict or peace researchers were intolerant and dismissive of the traditional approaches to these problems. The zeal of the newcomers bred intolerance among the traditionalists who naturally felt themselves threatened. They accepted the existence of war as an inescapable fact of the international system and sought to minimize its harmful effects through balance of power structures and the processes of international law.

Like the first Quakers with their religion, the conflict researchers with their science soon discovered the practical obstacles they had to face. The two schools are still healthily critical of each other, for that is the essential feature of intellectual progress, but their more intelligent adherents accept the value and insights of both approaches.[63]

The corporate responsibility of Friends
So far I have discussed the testimony of individual Friends whose concern over the problems arising from conflict and war leads them into various activities. Each one can only go as far as his conscience allows him and no one approach offers a complete solution. The Society has a corporate responsibility

towards its members so engaged, for their work will lose much of its strength and purpose unless it is informed by a spiritual quality.

Our corporate responsibility takes two forms: To offer the comfort of a spiritual home and the stimulus of a constant challenge to those whose work takes them far beyond the limits of the Quaker world and who are often lonely and isolated. If the Quaker message has any meaning at all, then it is the vision of a world transformed by Christ's love that grows in the heart of each and finds its fulfilment in our relations to one another. Friends seek to live this vision through the Meeting for Worship, through the conduct of their business and through their personal dealings with each other and with all people.

At one time, in the eighteenth and nineteenth centuries, Quakers formed an exclusive body which retained its identity through strict observance of various practices that distinguished it as a rather peculiar sect. The other-worldliness of Friends—though not in all respects, for they were often very successful in making money—had its use, for it kept alive a part of the vision which had so excited the first generation of Quakers.

Under the impact of world events during the past hundred years, Friends lost their sense of exclusiveness and ceased to be an inward-looking group. Perhaps not sufficiently, because outsiders are still inclined to regard us as rather strange people whose 'goodness' is not for them. I am always saddened when people tell me that they are not good enough to be Quakers. They have missed the point and that is largely because we seem to convey the wrong impression.

The core of the Society's corporate life is the Meeting for Worship. It is not a select gathering of the good or the saved. It is a fellowship of ordinary people endowed with a full share of human weaknesses, who seek to deepen their understanding by listening to the divine spirit that moves in all men. If the meeting is 'alive', a love will radiate out of the community and find expression in active service of all kinds.

G. M. Trevelyan once wrote that the essence of Quaker teaching was 'that Christian qualities matter much more than Christian dogmas'.[64] This conviction has led Friends in every generation to immerse themselves in the problems of their time. Their efforts have varied in direction and strength, depending largely upon historical circumstances. The present is a turbulent time in which we are very conscious of change and our restlessness is reflected in the many deliberations and disagreements within the Society. I think that there is still a basic unity among us, but we are obviously greatly troubled about the expression we should give to our vision. Much of the discussion still turns around the concepts of separate testimonies, like those of simplicity, social responsibility and peace.

When the affairs of men are in a state of flux, traditional boundaries break down. I have noted that the conditions of war and peace cannot be clearly separated, that social and international conflicts have become confused, that civilian and military affairs can no longer be easily distinguished, that it is difficult to say where domestic politics end and international politics begin. The redundance of old categories and compartments is paralleled by the redundance of any attempt to draw sharp distinctions between the different Quaker testimonies. Concerns over personal simplicity, poverty, social injustice, race relations, human rights, the proper use of resources, are all related to war and violence—and *vice-versa*.

The merging of all forms of Quaker witness brings us closer to the founders of the movement. They did things because they were dominated by a central vision. They thought of only one witness, not of separate testimonies. External factors both favour and hinder this trend today, for the blurring of traditional distinctions has been accompanied by an emphasis on expertise and specialization in every field of human activity.

We are bound to be slower in adapting the organization and structure of the Society to such changes. Sometimes I wonder whether it is wise to have permanent committees sitting in Friends House, looking for problems under different categories and deciding what should be done about them. There are far more problems than a tiny society can cope with. It might be better to devise a system whereby a small permanent staff services *ad hoc* committees that spring up as a result of concerns of individuals and groups. There should be more than enough concerns in a vigorous society. The main problem then will be to test their validity.

To provide the comfort of a spiritual home, it is, of course, necessary that the Society should be spiritually alive. The basic problem here is the old question which all religious groups have to face. How far should it be involved with the immediate problems of the day and how far should it stand apart? The obvious answer is that it should do both. Without immersion in contemporary affairs its message will become empty and meaningless. Too much immersion will cause it to lose a sense of perspective and consequently its message will lose depth and force.

The danger of institutionalization and too much bustle is balanced by the opposite danger of too much withdrawal. Looking at the state of the world and at the state of the Society of Friends, it is difficult to imagine that it can return to a quietist existence. On the other hand, it is impossible that Friends can make meaningful statements on every major issue without running the risk of losing sight of their basic message. The problem is not new. In 1909 there was discussion among English Friends as to what attitude to take towards the Territorial Forces Act. In view of the differences of opinion within the Society, Meeting for Sufferings came up with the following reference to the testimony against the un-Christian Spirit in all war:

> We are not called to enter on a crusade against the details of military preparations, but to deal with the whole question on spiritual and moral grounds.[65]

Surely, it will be objected, that is evading the specific issue. It is an escape into lofty sentiments and a refusal to come to grips with the immediate problems which affect our daily life. In confining their attention to the spiritual and moral realms, Friends are often accused of wanting to stand above the controversies and conflicts of the day, of refusing to take sides, of failing to stand up and be counted. One must admit the force of the criticism, and the behaviour of the Society at certain times in its history supports it. However, the failure to take sides on a particular issue need not mean neutrality, but that there is a third side; the side of Christ. George Fox had considerable experience of this problem as he was much abused by Parliamentarians and Royalists for refusing to be partisan.[66]

Individual members of the Society are constantly involved in current controversies and conflicts. Often they have to take sides. The effectiveness of their personal action will depend on the strength of their spiritual life, which is the primary concern of the Society.

That brings me to its second responsibility of constantly challenging its members to think through their position; to make them feel a little uncomfortable so that they do not become self-satisfied and complacent. They may be helped if the Society as a whole tries to relate the meaning of its vision of man's fulfilment to our understanding of the contemporary world. For, in the words of the second Swarthmore Lecture, the religious community has

> the duty of using its faculty of spiritual vision so as to penetrate below the surface of life to its inner meaning. Its

insight should lay bare the issues of good and evil that underlie the conventional morality and the current conduct of the time. Its faith should give it the courage to judge these issues from the standpoint of righteousness, but not by worldly policy, or the promptings of self-interest. The ideals of the Master are often regarded as impracticable in our unbrotherly world. But the Church is their natural guardian and has the mission of vindicating and realizing them.[67]

We recognize conflict as a fact of social life. Our task is to participate in it constructively and not to abolish it. In seeking a creative resolution, we have to accept the possibility of suffering and that our attempts may end in failure.

One form of suffering is personal. After centuries of tolerance and a remarkable degree of freedom, English and American Friends are inclined to forget the cost of being true to one's inner convictions. In 1948 I went to Holland to attend the first international meeting of Young Friends since the war. There I met a Swiss Friend who had been in and out of prison several times because of his refusal to bear arms. I was impressed how much easier it was to be a conscientious objector in England during the war than in Switzerland during peace. Sometimes one wonders for how much longer we shall enjoy so much freedom of conscience in this country. Fortunately, the early generations of Friends proved that the Light of Christ does not depend on the degree of tolerance in a state.

It is far more difficult to invite others to accept the consequence of actions which could lead to suffering. That is why it would be dishonest to advocate the way of non-violence and love without a reminder of the sacrifices which such a course may demand.

Those who prescribe some simple panacea to cure the world of war are false prophets. Disarmament, world government, technology, social revolution, alone, cannot save the world, for men are not gods. Disarmament makes little sense unless it is part of a general transformation of the international system. Attempts to establish universal empires have failed sooner or later through external pressures or internal decay. Technology leads to gross over-simplification of human problems and encourages a dangerous belief in man's omnipotence. The Revolution of 1789 with its magnificent slogan of Liberty, Equality, Fraternity, was followed by terror and the Napoleonic Empire; the communist revolution of 1917 by the tyranny of Stalin that left the state, which was to have withered away, stronger and more oppressive than ever before.

It is not the Society's task to pass judgement over its members, but it has a duty to help them submit to the judgement of their consciences, guided by the Light of Christ. To do this and to assist us in avoiding some of the pitfalls of our enthusiasm, Friends might turn to the practice of framing specific queries directed to all concerned with the problems of conflict and war.

Queries were originally requests for information about the state of the Society. Meetings were asked who had died or who were in prison and as to whether they had built Meeting Houses. As the Society became more settled in the early eighteenth century, they were aimed at ensuring greater consistency of conduct.

It is interesting that the first query to refer to warfare was not framed until 1742 and was combined with one about another matter. It asked:

> Do you bear a faithful and Christian testimony against the receiving or paying tithes? and against bearing of arms; and do you admonish such as are unfaithful therein?

It was not until a new formulation of the queries in 1860 that the testimony against bearing arms became the 'Christian Testimony against all war'.[68]

Today, we might ask those who work within the established system: In your eagerness to lay the foundations for a better world, are you in danger of placing too much reliance on institutions and procedures and too little on the promptings of the spirit? Are you too easily impressed by men of authority and reputation and not enough by ordinary men and women?

The following questions might be put to the revolutionaries among us: In your zeal for the cause, are you tempted to confuse self-righteousness with the righteousness of God? Does your hatred of the system and your struggle for justice lead you to think that the oppressor is the devil incarnate and not a human being like yourself? Are you inclined to think of non-violence as an end in itself rather than as an instrument in the service of love?

Finally, the thinkers and academics might be challenged thus: In your search for the causes of war and the conditions of peace, are you too much persuaded of your own intellectual powers and too little conscious of the limits of human reason? Do you mistake the findings of your studies and reflections for a practical contribution to the abolition of war? We might also put a supplementary question to the student of war: Are you so charmed by the gentlemanliness of the officers and by their reason that you forget the evil of war?

The first Friends had an apocalyptic vision of the world transformed by Christ and they set about to make it come true. The present generation of Quakers shares this conviction of the power of the spirit, but is doubtful whether it will transform the world in our lifetime, or in that of our children or children's children. For us it is not so important when the perfect world will be achieved or what it will be like. What matters is living our lives in the power of love and not worrying too much about the results. In doing this, the means become part of the end. Hence we lose the sense of helplessness and futility in the face of

101

the world's crushing problems. We also lose the craving for success, always focusing on the goal to the exclusion of the way of getting there. We must literally not take too much thought for the morrow but throw ourselves whole-heartedly into the present. That is the beauty of the way of love; it cannot be planned and its end cannot be foretold.

REFERENCES

Chapter I

[1] Lorenz (Konrad) *On Aggression*. Translated by Marjorie Latzke. London: Methuen, 1966, p. 186. Freud (Sigmund) *Why War?* International Institute of Intellectual Cooperation, 1933, quoted by Peter Mayer (ed.) *The Pacifist Conscience*. Harmondsworth: Penguin, 1966, pp. 243–4.

[2] For a discussion of the effect of Barclay's *Apology* on Quaker faith see the introduction by Rufus M. Jones in William C. Braithwaite's *The Second Period of Quakerism*. London: Macmillan, 1921, pp. xxx–xlv. For a full treatment of the whole problem of the interpretation of early Quaker teaching see Maurice A. Creasey *Early Quaker Christology* (Catholic and Quaker Studies No. 2, 1110 Wildwood Avenue, Manasquan, New Jersey 08736, USA) and the two review articles on it by Eva Pinthus 'Exploring our Roots' in *The Friend*, 16 and 23 November, 1973.

[3] See Edward Burrough's letter to the army in 1659 quoted in William C. Braithwaite *The Beginnings of Quakerism*. London: Macmillan, 1923, pp. 358–9.

[4] Quoted in Braithwaite *The Second Period of Quakerism*, p. 613.

[5] For a discussion of the spiritual origins of the Peace Testimony, see Rufus M. Jones *The Later Periods of Quakerism*. Vol. 1, London: Macmillan, 1921, pp. 156–7, and Hugh Barbour *The Quakers in Puritan England*. New Haven: Yale University Press. 1964, pp. 40, 163.

[6] Barbour, *op. cit.*, p. x.

[7] Wellock (Wilfred) *Peace News*. 24 September 1938.

[8] *Reconciliation*. **16**, October 1938, p. 289.

[9] *Peace News*. 11 June 1938.

[10] *A Declaration from the harmless and innocent People of God called Quakers, against all Plotters and Fighters in the World*. London: Robert Wilson, 1660, pp. 3, 1–2.

[11] There is no reference to 'Peace Testimony' in the index of Braithwaite's *The Beginnings of Quakerism*. Only to 'WAR, testimony against'.

[12] *Ibid.*, p. 462.

[13] London Yearly Meeting Epistle, 14–19 March, 1744. *Epistles from the Yearly Meeting of Friends held in London*. Vol. 1, London: Edward Marsh. Friends' Book and Tract Depository, 1858, p. 247. The last sentence finishes with a quotation from *Isaiah*, ix, 7.

[14] London Yearly Meeting Epistle, 1805. *Extracts from the Minutes and Advices of the Yearly Meeting of Friends held in London from its first Institution*. 2nd edn. with supplement. London: James Phillips, 1822, pp. 296–7.

[15] London Yearly Meeting Epistle, 23 May–1 June, 1804. *Epistles from the Yearly Meeting of Friends held in London*. Vol. 2, pp. 123–4.

[16] London Yearly Meeting Epistle, 20–30 May, 1846. *Ibid.*, p. 333.

[17] Moulton (Phillips P.) ed., *The Journal and Major Essays of John Woolman*. New York: Oxford University Press, 1971, p. 75.

[18] Arendt (Hannah) *On Violence*. London: Allen Lane, the Penguin Press, 1970, p. 22.

[19] *The Friend*, 28 January 1910, pp. 52–4.

[20] Nuttall (Geoffrey) *Christian Pacifism in History*. Oxford: Basil Blackwell, 1958, reprinted by World without War Council, Berkeley, California, 1971, p. 3.

Chapter II

[21] Cole (Alan) 'The Social Origins of Early Friends' in *Journal of Friends' Historical Society*, **48**, 3, 1957, p. 118.

[22] Barbour, *op. cit.*, p. 221.

[23] *Ibid.*, p. 254.

[24] Paper submitted by John Whitehead and George Whitehead to William III on 8 April 1696, quoted in Margaret E. Hirst *The Quakers in Peace and War: an account of their peace principles and practice*. London: Swarthmore Press, 1923, pp. 108–9.

[25] Barclay (Robert) A lover and travailer for the peace of Christendom. *An Epistle of Love and Friendly Advice, etc.*, delivered on 23 and 24 February 1677–8. London: Benjamin Clark, 1679, pp. 13–14.

[26] Wood (J. Duncan) *Building the Institutions of Peace*. Swarthmore Lecture 1962. London: Allen & Unwin, 1962.

[27] Penn (William) *An Essay Towards the Present and Future Peace of Europe, by the Establishment of an European Dyet, Parliament, or Estates*. London, 1693, pp. 4–5.

[28] Byberry (John and Isaac Comly) eds. 'Anecdotes and Memoirs of Warner Mifflin' in *Friends' Miscellany*. Philadelphia: J. Richards, 1834, **5**, p. 222.

[29] For discussions of the impact of the American Civil War, see Hirst *op. cit.*, pp. 422–48, and Jones, *op. cit.*, vol. 2, pp. 728–53.

[30] For an analysis and critique of the liberal view, see Kenneth Waltz *Man, the State and War*. New York: Columbia University Press, paperback edition, 1970, pp. 95–114.

[31] Frick (Stephen) 'The *Christian Appeal* of 1855: Friends' Public Response to the Crimean War' in *Journal of Friends' Historical Society*, **52**, 2, 1970, pp. 203–10.

[32] Frick (Stephen) 'The Quaker Deputation to Russia: January–February 1854' in *Journal of Friends' Historical Society*, **52**, 2, 1969, pp. 80–1.

[33] Byrd (Robert O.) *Quaker Ways in Foreign Policy*. Toronto: University of Toronto Press, 1960, p. 144.

[34] Heath (Carl) *Quaker Embassies*. Published privately by the author, Oxted, Surrey, n.d., p. 2. There is a sympathetic but critical account of the work of the Quaker Embassies in Bertram Pickard *Pacifist Diplomacy in Conflict Situations*. Philadelphia: Pacifist Research Bureau, 1943.

[35] *The Friend*, 24 October 1941.

[36] Bailey (Sydney D.) *Prohibitions and Restraints in War*. London: The Royal Institute of International Affairs. Oxford University Press, 1972, pp. 20–3.

[37] Moulton, *op. cit.*, p. 88.

[38] Rogers (James E.) ed. *John Bright, M.P., Speeches on Questions of Public Policy*. Vol. 2. London: Macmillan, 1868, p. 397.

[39] Quoted in Hirst, *op. cit.*, p. 421.

[40] *Conference of All Friends Held in London, August 12–20, 1920, Official Report*. London: Published for the Conference Continuation Committee by Friends Bookshop, 1920, p. 201.

Chapter III

[41] Wright (Quincy) *A Study of War*. Abridged edn. Chicago: University of Chicago Press, 1964.

[42] Bettelheim (Bruno) *The Informed Heart: the human condition in mass society*. London: Granada Publishing, Paladin, 1970, pp. 52–4.

[43] For a development of this concept, see John W. Burton *International Relations: a general theory*. London: Cambridge University Press, 1965, pp. 1–2, 149–50, 178.

[44] See particularly Herman Kahn *On Thermonuclear War*. Princeton, N.J.: Princeton University Press, 1960; *Thinking about the Unthinkable*. London: Weidenfeld, 1962; *On Escalation: metaphors and scenarios*. London: Pall Mall Press, 1965.

[45] Buchan (Alastair) 'A World Restored?' in *Foreign Affairs*, July 1972, p. 650.

[46] The problems raised by the participation of scientists in policy-making are fully discussed in Robert Gilpin *American Scientists and Nuclear Weapons Policy*. Princeton, N.J.: Princeton University Press, 1962.

[47] Schelling (Thomas C.) *The Strategy of Conflict*. Cambridge, Mass: Harvard University Press, 1963; with Morton H. Halperin *Strategy and Arms Control*. New York: Twentieth Century Fund, 1961.

[48] Green (Philip) *Deadly Logic: the theory of nuclear deterrence*. Ohio State University Press, 1966, especially pp. 36–7, 89–90, 149, 195, 213–6, 221–47, 263. Green is weak on alternatives to nuclear deterrence. For attacks on his support of minimum deterrence and his vague idealism see Paul D. Wolfowitz 'The Pot and the Kettle, or Rationality within Reason: Mr. Green's Deadly Logic' and Paul Ramsey 'A Political Ethics Context for Strategic Thinking' in Morton A. Kaplan *Strategic Thinking and its Moral Implications*. University of Chicago, Center for Policy Study, 1973, pp. 69–100, 119–30.

[49] Wood (David) *Conflict in the Twentieth Century*. London: Institute for Strategic Studies. Adelphi Paper 48, June 1968, pp. 1, 19.

[50] Hart (B. H. Liddell) *Strategy: the indirect approach*. Revised edn. London: Faber, 1967, p. 335.

[51] See particularly André Beaufre *Stratégie de L'Action*. Paris: Armand Colin, 1966, translated by R. H. Barry *Strategy of Action*. London: Faber, 1967.

[52] Huntington (Samuel P.) *The Soldier and the State: the theory and politics of civil-military relations*. New York: Vintage Books, a Caravelle edition, 1964, p. 79.

[53] *Weissbuch 1970 zur Sicherheit der Bundesrepublik Deutschland und zur Lage der Bundeswehr*. Bonn: Presse und Informationsamt der Bundesregierung, 1970, pp. 121–7.

[54] Andreski (Stanislav) *Military Organization and Society*. Revised edn. London: Routledge, 1968, pp. 184–6.

Chapter IV
[55] Barnes (Kenneth C.) *The Creative Imagination*. Swarthmore Lecture 1960. London: Allen & Unwin, 1960, paperback reprint Friends Home Service Committee, 1969.

[56] For an excellent discussion of the subject, see Sydney Bailey *Prohibitions and Restraints in War, op. cit.*

[57] Ishida (Takeshi) 'Beyond the Traditional Concepts of Peace in Different Cultures' in *Journal of Peace Research*. Oslo: Peace Research Institute, Universitets Forlaget, 1969, No. 5, pp. 133–45, especially pp. 134–5.

[58] Roberts (Adam) ed. *The Strategy of Civilian Defence: non-violent resistance to aggression*. London: Faber, 1967.

[59] Tanzer (Michael) *The Political Economy of International Oil and the Underdeveloped Countries*. Boston: Beacon Press, 1969, pp. 26–7.

[60] de Montesquieu (Baron) *The Spirit of the Laws*. Book 1, chapter 3. Translated by Thomas Nugent. New York: Hafner, 1966, p. 5.

[61] Richardson (Lewis Fry) *Statistics of Deadly Quarrels* edited by Quincy Wright and C. C. Lienau. London: Stevens, 1960; *Arms and Insecurity* edited by Nicolas Rashevsky and Ernesto Trucco. London: Stevens, 1960.

[62] Coser (Lewis) *The Functions of Social Conflict*. London: Routledge, 1965, pp. 151–7.

[63] For a comprehensive survey of the many different schools of international theory, see Joseph Frankel *Contemporary International Theory and the Behaviour of States*. London: Oxford University Press, 1973.

[64] Trevelyan (G. M.) *English Social History*. London: Longmans, 1945, p. 267.

[65] *The Friend*, 8 January 1909.

[66] Nickalls (John L.) ed. *The Journal of George Fox*. London: Cambridge University Press, 1952, pp. xxix, 65, 67, 379–82, 398–404, 693.

[67] Braithwaite (William C.) *Spiritual Guidance in the Experience of the Society of Friends*. Swarthmore Lecture. London: Headley Brothers, 1909, p. 103.

[68] Stagg (Richard E.) 'Friends' Queries and General Advices' in *Journal of the Friends' Historical Society*, **49**, 4, 1961, pp. 209–14, 230; **49**, 5, 1961, p. 251.